COMPASS
CONSTRUCTIONS

COMPASS CONSTRUCTIONS

ACTIVITIES FOR USING A COMPASS AND STRAIGHTEDGE

Christopher M. Freeman

PRUFROCK PRESS INC.
WACO, TEXAS

Edited by Jennifer Robins
Production Design by Marjorie Parker

ISBN-13: 978-1-59363-316-5
ISBN-10: 1-59363-316-5

Prufrock Press Inc.
P.O. Box 8813
Waco, TX 76714-8813
Phone: (800) 998-2208
Fax: (800) 240-0333
http://www.prufrock.com

Dedication

This book is dedicated to my wife, Maria, with gratitude for her tireless support and confidence, and to our children, all of whom love constructions: to Clara, whose eagerness with the first lessons convinced me of their value; to Edward, who liked constructions so well, he took his compass with him on vacation; and to John, who someday will draw his constructions in the finished book.

Contents

Acknowledgements

Thanks to Hanna Goldschmidt, mentor, colleague, and friend, under whose direction I first taught geometry; to Bobbi Nelson, fellow geometry teacher, who eagerly adopted these lessons into her classes, made valuable suggestions, and encouraged me to write more; to Paul Gunty, Shirley Holbrook, and all of my colleagues for their ideas and inspiration; to Joan Franklin Smutny, Director of the Center for Gifted at National-Louis University, for her perennial encouragement; to Gretchen Sparling and Jennifer Robins at Prufrock Press for their excellent suggestions; and to the hundreds of children in the "Worlds of Wisdom and Wonder" programs and at The University of Chicago Laboratory Schools who enjoyed these lessons and helped me improve them.

Introduction

Compass Constructions provides hands-on activities to supplement a high school geometry text or to differentiate instruction for gifted middle school students. Students will work eagerly on these constructions while learning and applying fundamental geometric principles. The construction activities in this book promote success in a formal, proof-oriented geometry class.

A construction is a procedure for creating a geometric figure, such as the bisector of an angle or a regular hexagon. For thousands of years, students have used two simple tools to draw constructions: a straightedge to draw lines and a compass to draw arcs and copy distances. Geometric principles ensure that the procedures create perfect figures in theory, and students enjoy constructing precise drawings in practice.

The activities in this book reinforce and utilize the fundamental concepts that are studied in middle and high school geometry classes, such as the definitions and properties of angle bisectors, perpendicular bisectors, parallel lines with transversals, parallelograms and other special quadrilaterals, congruent and similar triangles, circles, and tangents. Students also will broaden their knowledge beyond the standard curriculum by investigating topics such as the Golden Ratio, Construction Arithmetic, and Hilbert's Theorem.

Suggested Grade Levels

This activity book is intended for students of high school geometry or students in grades 5–8. It also has been used successfully with advanced math students in younger grades.

Students studying high school geometry enjoy these construction activities as a hands-on application of the fundamental concepts they study in class. The chapter on Constructing Triangles is especially valuable for students as they study triangle congruence: When students have constructed a triangle using Side-Angle-Side (SAS), they are better equipped to understand why SAS can prove two triangles congruent.

Students in grades 5–8 enjoy Chapters 1–5 as a way to develop a new set of skills. Students readily appreciate the opportunity to discern the properties of geometric shapes, and these activities prepare students for success in a formal, proof-oriented geometry class later. The NCTM *Focal Points* emphasize that elementary school students need to develop geometric intuition in math class through drawing and analyzing two-dimensional figures; this is precisely what these lessons accomplish.

Gifted students in Grades 3–4 also thoroughly enjoy the construction activities in Chapters 1–5. The lessons are designed for students to work independently, thus allowing students to proceed at their own pace and learn the concepts in depth.

These lessons have been tested with students of various age levels, and revisions have been made to make the lessons self-explanatory. All students find constructions a fun way to deepen their understanding of geometry.

How to Use This Book

High school students may work on these lessons concurrently with appropriate chapters in their textbook. Middle school students may work on these activities independently, making this book useful for either curriculum compacting or pull-out gifted education settings.

On the first day of instruction, it is important to demonstrate proper use of the compass and straightedge. Hold the compass at the top, not by the pencil. Use the other hand to press the sharp point against the paper. To make a smooth arc, lean the compass in the direction that you are moving it. To be more accurate, draw light arcs. Many students also need practice using a ruler to draw a line through the centers of two pictured points. Encourage precision!

With my high school geometry students, I devote a class day to Chapter 1, Lines and Arcs. I devote the next two class days to Chapter 6, Constructing Triangles, because my textbook introduces triangle congruence quite early. (To avoid confusion, I save the lesson on Side-Side-Angle [SSA] for later.) I assign the other *Compass Construction* chapters in sequence, coinciding with the appropriate chapters of the textbook. Students complete their constructions at home.

With younger students, I devote 2 weeks of class time to drawing constructions. After I demonstrate proper technique, I let the students work at their own pace, lesson by lesson. Students turn in their daily work, and I check each construction for correct procedure and precision. During class, I work with individual students, reviewing procedures as necessary and sometimes requesting a student to redraw a construction.

Materials Needed

Each student will need a ruler and a compass. Choose a compass that is easy to adjust but will maintain a constant radius while being used. I provide compasses for students to use in class, but I suggest that each student purchase a higher quality compass (approximately $10) for his or her own use at home. My own compass has lasted 25 years.

Assessment

For high school geometry students, I give each construction a point value (1, 2, or 3 points). The answers to questions are worth half-points. Each chapter is assigned as a separate packet, which may be worth from 10–40 points. Constructions are a separate grade category, worth 10% of the final grade.

For younger students, I provide individual lessons for students to work on at their own pace. I check each lesson for precision. Each lesson gets a grade of √, +, or ++ (one plus for correct procedure, one for precision). Students strive a little harder to receive two plusses! Some lessons, such as the Regular Dodecagon, make striking bulletin board displays, which provide additional motivation for students to work with care.

NCTM Standards

The activities in *Compass Constructions* fulfill national education standards set by the National Council of Teachers of Mathematics.

Geometry Standard 1 expects all students to analyze various geometric shapes, to formulate conjectures about their characteristic properties, and to reason logically to justify these conjectures. Every construction activity in this book fulfills this standard. Constructions provide a *purpose* for geometric inquiry: One needs to understand the properties of a figure to be able correctly to construct it.

Geometry Standard 4 expects high school students to construct geometric figures using a variety of tools. It is to be hoped that every geometry student also has the opportunity to utilize computer software for constructing geometric figures, such as The Geometer's Sketchpad or Cabri. My own geometry students use computers extensively in class. But, I have found that students find it even more satisfying to draw their constructions by hand.

Prerequisite Guidance

Students like to draw constructions with precision. Ensure that their straightedges are really straight, that their compasses hold a fixed radius, and that their pencils are sharp. Ensure that students hold their compasses correctly, by the top and not by the pencil point. Remind them to draw lightly, because a thin line or arc is much more precise than a thick one. If a construction is poorly done, I sometimes erase it and request the student to try again. Once students develop good technique, they become very independent.

A Final Word

Hundreds of my own students have loved these construction activities. I have written this book so that you and your students will enjoy them, too.

Chapter 1:
Lines and Arcs

Name_____   Date_____

Introduction: The Straightedge and Compass Tools

For more than 2,000 years, mathematicians have used two basic tools to construct geometric figures: a **compass** to draw circles, and a **straightedge** to draw lines. With these simple tools, you will learn to construct triangles, hexagons, squares, kites, perpendicular lines, parallel lines, and lots of other figures.

A compass has a sharp point at one end to hold it steady at the center of the circle, and it has a pencil point at the other end to draw the circle. The distance between the sharp point and the pencil point is called the **radius**. You will use a compass to draw circles and arcs. To draw a straight line, you will pull a pencil tip along a straightedge. A straightedge is different from a ruler, because a straightedge has no marks on it. If you use a ruler, you should ignore the inch or centimeter markings. To measure length, you will use the radius of the compass.

Lesson 1.1
Construct a Circle by Center and Point

A point is a location. We often represent a point with a dot (.), but any dot is really too big because the point is at the center of the dot. We name points with capital letters, like points C and P below.

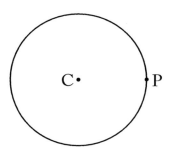

One way to construct a circle starts with one point that will be its center and another point that will be on the circle. Follow the directions below to construct the circle with center C and passing through P. Your construction will look like the picture to the right.

1. Put the sharp point of the compass onto C and hold it there.

2. Adjust the compass radius so that the pencil point rests gently on the point P.

3. Hold the compass at its top, not by the pencil

4. Lean the compass slightly in the direction you want to draw.

5. Start drawing the circle through P; if the curve doesn't go exactly through the center of point P, adjust the radius and start again.

6. Lightly draw the circle with your compass.

•
C

•
P

Lesson 1.2
Construct a Line and an Equilateral Triangle

A basic postulate of geometry is that *two points determine a line.* In practice, drawing this line is not as trivial as it may sound. If you work carefully, your construction will look like the picture below. Follow the directions below to construct a line.

1. Place your straightedge *just under* the two points P and Q below. Hold it steady.

2. As you pull your pencil along the straightedge, make sure that the pencil tip goes through the *center* of each point. If not, change the angle of your pencil, or adjust your straightedge. Be precise! Make sure your pencil is sharp.

3. Draw an arrowhead at each end of your line.

The arrowheads indicate that **lines** go on forever in both directions. We name a line using any two points on it with a line symbol above them, such as $\overleftrightarrow{PQ}$. The piece of a line between two **endpoints** (like P and Q above) is called a **line segment**, or **segment** for short. We name a segment using its two endpoints with a bar on top, such as $\overline{PQ}$. Segments don't go on forever, they end at their endpoints.

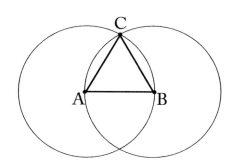

Now you will construct an **equilateral triangle,** in which all three sides are segments of equal length. Your construction will look like the picture to the right.

1. Use your straightedge to construct the line segment $\overline{AB}$.

2. Construct a circle with center A and passing through B.

3. Construct another circle with center B and passing through A.

4. Locate a point where the two circles intersect and label it C. (You don't need to draw a dot because the location where two circles cross *is* a point.)

5. Use your straightedge to construct segments $\overline{AC}$ and $\overline{BC}$. You now have equilateral $\triangle ABC$!

.
A

.
B

Lesson 1.3
Draw an Arc and Copy a Segment

Just as a segment is a piece of a line, an **arc** is a piece of a circle.
Which point, A, B, or C, is the **center of the arc** shown below? _____

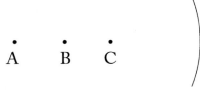

To check your answer, put the sharp point of your compass on A, adjust your radius, and try to draw the arc. Then put the sharp point on B and try to draw the arc. Then repeat using point C. (Was your answer correct?)

To **copy a segment** means to make another segment with the same length. Don't use a ruler to measure length—use the radius of your compass! When you follow the directions below, you will construct a copy of segment $\overline{EF}$, called $\overline{PQ}$. Your construction will look like this picture:

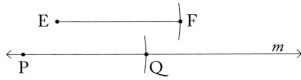

Use segment $\overline{EF}$ and line m, below.
1. Anywhere on the line m, mark a tiny dot and label it P.
2. Put the sharp point of your compass on E, and adjust the radius so you can draw a short arc through F.
3. Don't change the radius, but move the sharp point to P and draw a short arc that crosses line m.
4. Label the point where the arc crosses the line, Q.
5. $\overline{PQ}$ is a copy of $\overline{EF}$, because it has the same length.

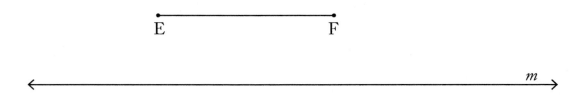

When we *name* a segment, we put a bar on top, as with $\overline{PQ}$. When we refer to the *length* of a segment, we don't put a bar on top. Thus "PQ" means the length of $\overline{PQ}$, which is the distance from P to Q. Because PQ and EF are numbers, we can write PQ = EF to mean that the segments have the same length.

Lesson 1.4
Construct Equally Spaced Concentric Circles

Concentric circles have the same center. If they are equally spaced, they will look like a target, as shown to the right. To construct these circles, we don't need the entire line $\overleftrightarrow{CD}$, we just need the part of the line that starts at C and extends to the right through D and beyond. A part of a line that has one endpoint but extends infinitely far in the other direction is called a **ray**. Rays are named with the endpoint first, some other point on the ray second, and a ray symbol on top. The ray we need for the construction of the following concentric circles is named $\overrightarrow{CD}$.

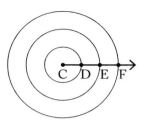

Follow the directions below to construct equally spaced concentric circles.

1. Use your straightedge to construct the ray $\overrightarrow{CD}$, starting at C and passing through D and beyond to the edge of the page.

2. Draw the circle with center C and passing through D.

3. Keeping the radius CD, draw a short arc with center D and crossing the ray on the right side of D. Label the intersection point E.

4. Keeping the same radius, draw a short arc with center E and crossing the ray on the right side of E. Label the intersection point F.

5. Draw the circle with center C and passing through E.

6. Draw the circle with center C and passing through F.

C   D

Lesson 1.5
Construct a Regular Hexagon

A **regular hexagon** has six equal sides and six equal angles. Six equilateral triangles fit together to form a regular hexagon.

Your challenge is to figure out how to construct a regular hexagon, called HEXAGO, when given one side, $\overline{HE}$. The picture to the right shows just the hexagon and triangles, it does not show the circles or arcs needed to construct it.

Don't try to draw a hexagon with just a straightedge! You will need to use your compass to draw circles or arcs in order to put the points N, O, G, A, and X in their proper places. As you work, *never erase construction arcs!* Leave your arcs to illustrate your method.

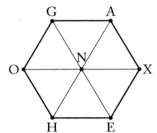

Hint: Use the method shown in Lesson 1.2 to construct equilateral triangle ΔHEN. Then construct equilateral triangle ΔENX. Continue to construct each of the remaining triangles.

H •———————————————————• E

Chapter 2:
Kites and Basic
Constructions

Lesson 2.1
Construct an Isosceles Triangle and a Kite

A triangle is called **isosceles** when at least two of its sides are the same length. The third side is called the **base**. Follow the directions below to construct isosceles ΔKIT with base $\overline{KT}$ and two sides equal to $\overline{MN}$. Your construction will look like the example to the right.

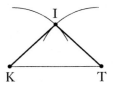

1. Draw a short arc with center M passing through N. This will ensure that the compass radius is set at $\overline{MN}$.

2. Keeping radius MN, draw a long arc with center K, above and to the right of K.

3. Keeping radius MN, draw a long arc with center T, above and to the left of T.

4. Label the point where the arcs cross, I.

5. Draw $\overline{KI}$ and $\overline{TI}$. KI = TI, making ΔKIT isosceles!

M •————————• N

K •————————————• T

If you draw two isosceles triangles with the same base, then the pairs of equal sides form a **kite**, as shown in the example to the right. Follow the directions below to finish drawing kite KITE, still using $\overline{KT}$ above.

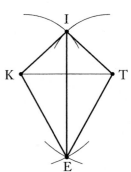

6. Open your compass to a wider radius of your choice.

7. Draw an arc with center K, below and to the right of K.

8. Draw an arc with center T, below and to the left of T.

9. Label the point where the two arcs cross, E.

10. Draw $\overline{KE}$ and $\overline{TE}$. KE = TE, making KITE a kite!

11. Also draw $\overline{IE}$. $\overline{KT}$ and $\overline{IE}$ are called **diagonals** of KITE. A diagonal of a kite is a segment that connects opposite corners.

Lesson 2.2
Two Special Kites: A Rhombus and a Non-Convex Kite

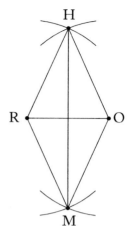

A kite that has four equal sides is called a **rhombus**. Follow the directions below to construct rhombus RHOM, as in the picture to the right.

1. Open your compass to any radius you like. Construct an isosceles triangle above $\overline{RO}$.

2. Construct another isosceles triangle the same size below $\overline{RO}$.

3. Label the top point H and the bottom point M. RHOM is a rhombus.

4. Draw the other diagonal, $\overline{HM}$.

R •————————————• O

Both kites you have drawn so far are **convex**: one isoceles triangle is above and the other is below their common base. If both triangles are on the same side of their common base, the kite is called **nonconvex**. Now you will construct a nonconvex kite.

5. Using any radius you choose, construct an isosceles triangle above base $\overline{KT}$.

6. Change your compass radius, and construct another isosceles triangle—also above base $\overline{KT}$.

7. Label the new corner points I and E.

8. Draw the diagonal $\overline{IE}$.

K •——————————————• T

How are the diagonals of a nonconvex kite different from those of a convex kite?

_____

_____

_____

Lesson 2.3
Useful Properties of Kites

As you know, a kite is formed from two isosceles triangles with a common base. These triangles may be tipped sideways, as in the picture to the right. The common base, $\overline{KT}$, is one diagonal of a kite. The other diagonal is called the **main diagonal,** $\overline{EI}$. The main diagonal of a kite has several properties that are used extensively in constructions. See if you can discover them.

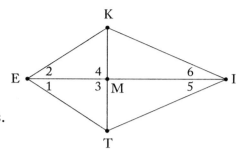

Circle your answers to the following questions:

a. What type of angle is angle 4: acute, right, or obtuse?

b. Which length is longer: KM, TM, or are they equal?

c. Which angle is wider: angle 1, angle 2, or are they equal?

d. Which angle is wider: angle 5, angle 6, or are they equal?

You may have discovered several properties of the main diagonal of any kite. We will use them often in constructions. Learn them!

1. The diagonals of a kite are **perpendicular**, because they form right angles. (Did you find that angle 4 is a right angle?)

2. The main diagonal of a kite contains the **midpoint** of the other diagonal. (Did you find that M was exactly in the middle of $\overline{KT}$?)

3. The main diagonal is thus the **perpendicular bisector** of the other diagonal. (To *bisect* means "to cut into two equal pieces.")

4. The main diagonal is the **angle bisector** of each angle. (Did you find that angle 1 was equal to angle 2, and also that angle 5 was equal to angle 6?)

Appendix A provides a formal proof that the diagonals of a kite have these properties.

Lesson 2.4
Construct the Midpoint of a Segment Using Its Perpendicular Bisector

The **perpendicular bisector** of a segment is a line that contains the midpoint of the segment and is perpendicular to the segment. To construct the perpendicular bisector, simply construct the main diagonal of a kite. Your construction will look like the example to the right.

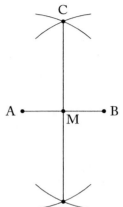

1. Open the compass to any radius greater than half the length of $\overline{AB}$. (An easy radius to use is AB itself.)

2. Draw an arc with center A, above and to the right of A.

3. Keeping the same radius, draw an arc with center B, above and to the left of B.

4. Label the point where the two arcs intersect, C.

5. Draw two more arcs with the same radius (one with center A and the other with center B) that intersect *below* segment $\overline{AB}$. Label this intersection D.

6. Use the straightedge to draw $\overline{CD}$. $\overline{CD}$ is the **perpendicular bisector** of $\overline{AB}$.

7. The point where $\overline{CD}$ crosses $\overline{AB}$ is the **midpoint** of $\overline{AB}$. Label it M.

8. On the picture in the upper right corner of the page, lightly draw all four sides of kite ACBD; $\overline{CD}$ is its main diagonal.

Lesson 2.5
Construct a Square When Given Its Diagonal

A **square** is a special type of kite that has four equal sides and four equal angles. The four corners of a square lie on a circle. See the example to the right.

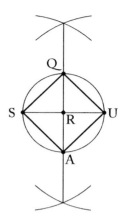

Using $\overline{SU}$ below as a diagonal, construct a square following the directions below.

1. Construct the perpendicular bisector of $\overline{SU}$. (Follow the procedure you learned in Lesson 2.4.)

2. Label the midpoint of $\overline{SU}$, R.

3. Draw a circle with center R and passing through S.

4. Label the points where the circle crosses the perpendicular bisector, Q and A.

5. Use your straightedge to draw $\overline{SQ}$, $\overline{UQ}$, $\overline{SA}$, and $\overline{UA}$. SQUA is a square!

S •————————————————————————————• U

Lesson 2.6
Bisect an Angle

An **angle** is made up of two rays with a common endpoint. The rays are called the **sides** of the angle. The endpoint is called the **vertex** of the angle. We often use the vertex point to name the angle; for example, the angle in the middle of this page called "angle B."

    To **bisect** an angle means to draw a ray that splits the angle into two equal angles. The ray is called an **angle bisector.** Our angle bisector will be the main diagonal of a kite. Follow the directions below to bisect angle B.

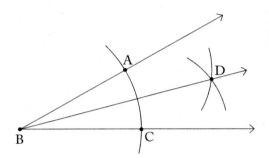

1. Draw an arc with center B and a radius of your choice, but not too small. Label the points where the arc crosses each side of the angle, A and C.

2. Draw an arc with center A.

3. With the same radius, draw an arc with center C.

4. Label the point where the two arcs cross, D.

5. Draw a ray from B through D. This ray bisects angle B. (Imagine drawing $\overline{AD}$ and $\overline{CD}$. Do you see that BADC would be a kite?)

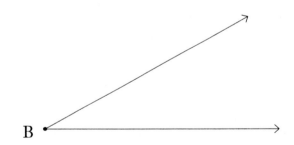

6. Now, use the same procedure to bisect right angle P below.

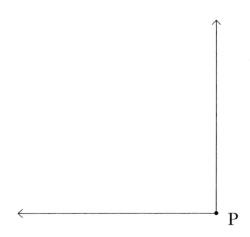

Lesson 2.7
Construct a Regular Octagon

A **regular octagon** has eight equal sides and eight equal angles. Like a square, all of the corners of a regular octagon lie on a circle. Your construction will look like the one to the right.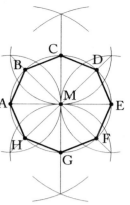

1. Construct the perpendicular bisector of $\overline{AE}$. (Remember Lesson 2.4?)

2. Label the midpoint of $\overline{AE}$, M.

3. Draw a circle with center M and passing through A.

4. Label the points where the circle crosses the perpendicular bisector, C and G.

Note: The point M is the vertex of four right angles. One of them has sides $\overrightarrow{MA}$ and $\overrightarrow{MC}$. In steps 5–7, you will construct the angle bisector of this right angle.

5. Draw a long arc with center A and passing through M.

6. Draw a long arc with center C and passing through M. Be sure that the two arcs cross. (Do you see that this crossing point, and A, M, and C, are corners of a kite?)

7. Draw the angle bisector from M through the intersection of those two arcs.

8. Label the point where the circle with center M intersects the angle bisector, B.

9. Use the method of steps 5–8 to construct the angle bisectors of each of the other three right angles with vertex M. (You will construct a 4-petal flower, too; if you wish, color in the petals with colored pencils!)

10. Label the points where the circle with center M intersects these angle bisectors, D, F, and H.

11. Connect the eight points on the circle to form regular octagon ABCDEFGH.

A •————————————————————• E

Lesson 2.8
Construct a Regular Dodecagon (Clock)

Look back at the construction of a regular octagon in Lesson 2.7. Ignore the angle bisectors, ignore the points B, D, F, and H, and ignore the octagon. Can you see how the arcs you drew form four petals of a flower? Can you see how to draw those petals using just four long arcs? These arcs, together with the vertical and horizontal line segments, cross the circle with center M in 12 equally spaced points. These points form the vertices of a regular dodecagon.

On segment $\overline{AG}$ below, recreate the construction of the four petals. Omit the angle bisectors, and omit the octagon. Locate the 12 points equally spaced around the circle, and construct a **regular dodecagon**—a polygon with 12 equal sides and 12 angles. Decorate your dodecagon with the numbers of a clock (1–12).

A  G

Chapter 3:
Centers of a Triangle

Lesson 3.1
Drop a Perpendicular

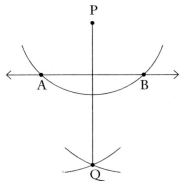

Imagine dropping a ball onto the floor. The ball will fall in a line that is perpendicular to the floor. In the diagram, point P represents the ball, and the given line represents the floor. Through point P, we will construct a line that is perpendicular to the given line. This perpendicular will be the main diagonal of a kite.

1. Open the compass to any convenient radius that is greater than the distance between P and the line.

2. Draw an arc with center P that crosses the line in two points. Label these points A and B. (Imagine connecting $\overline{PA}$ and $\overline{PB}$ to form an isosceles triangle.)

3. Draw an arc with center A, below and to the right of A.

4. Keeping the same radius, draw another arc with center B, below and to the left of B.

5. Label the point where the two arcs cross, Q.

6. Draw $\overline{PQ}$, which is perpendicular to the line.

7. On the sample diagram above, draw kite PBQA. Do you see that $\overline{PQ}$ is the main diagonal of kite PBQA?

P .

Lesson 3.2
Centers of a Triangle I: Altitudes

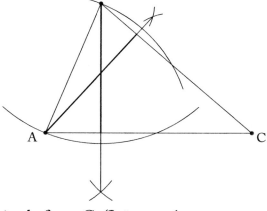

In any triangle, if you drop a perpendicular from a vertex to the opposite side, the segment you construct is called an **altitude**. The altitudes from A and from B are shown in the sample diagram to the right. The altitude from C is not shown.

1. Drop a perpendicular from B to $\overline{AC}$. This is the altitude from B. (Use the method shown in Lesson 3.1.)

2. Drop a perpendicular from A to $\overline{BC}$. This is the altitude from A.

3. Drop a perpendicular from C to $\overline{AB}$. This is the altitude from C. (It is not shown in the sample diagram, but you can construct it using the same method.)

4. If you have worked very carefully, the three altitudes should intersect at a single point. (If they don't, find your mistake and fix it!) Label that point the **orthocenter**. (*Ortho-* means "right" or "straight." For example, an orthodontist straightens teeth. Because altitudes intersect sides at right angles, the intersection point of the altitudes is called the orthocenter.)

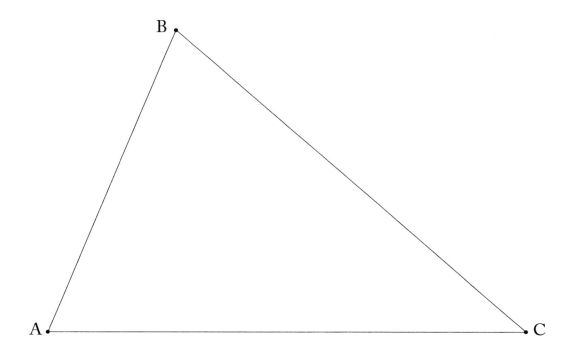

Lesson 3.3
Centers of a Triangle II: Angle Bisectors

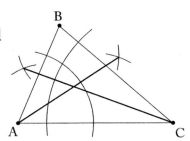

The three angle bisectors of a triangle also meet at one point, called the **incenter**. The angle bisectors from A and from C are shown at right.

1. Construct the angle bisector of angle A. (Use the method shown in Lesson 2.6.)

2. Construct the angle bisector of angle C.

3. Construct the angle bisector of angle B. (It is not shown in the sample picture, but you can construct it using the same method.)

4. If you have worked very carefully, all three angle bisectors should meet at a single point. (If they don't, find your mistake and fix it!) Label this point the **incenter**. (It is the center of the **inscribed circle**, which you will draw in steps 5 and 6.)

5. Drop a perpendicular from the incenter to side $\overline{AC}$. Label the point where this perpendicular crosses $\overline{AC}$, P. (This construction is shown at left. Use the method shown in Lesson 3.1.)

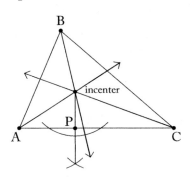

6. Draw the circle with center at the incenter and passing through P. This circle should just touch all three sides of the triangle. (*Scribe* means "to write" or "to draw." The **inscribed circle** is drawn inside the triangle.)

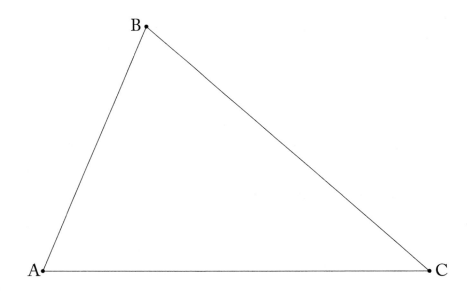

Lesson 3.4
Centers of a Triangle III: Perpendicular Bisectors

1. Construct the **perpendicular bisector** of $\overline{BC}$, as shown in the example to the right. (Use the method shown in Lesson 2.4.)

2. Using the same method, construct the perpendicular bisectors of sides $\overline{AB}$ and $\overline{AC}$.

3. The three perpendicular bisectors should meet at a single point. (If they don't, find your mistake and fix it!) Label this point the **circumcenter**. (It is the center of the **circumscribed circle**.)

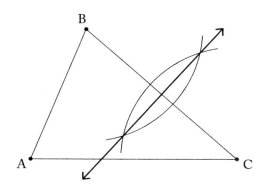

4. Draw the circle with center at the circumcenter and passing through A. *This circle should pass through points A, B, and C. (Circum-* means "around." For example, Magellan's expedition circumnavigated, or sailed around, the world. The **circumscribed circle** is drawn around the triangle.)

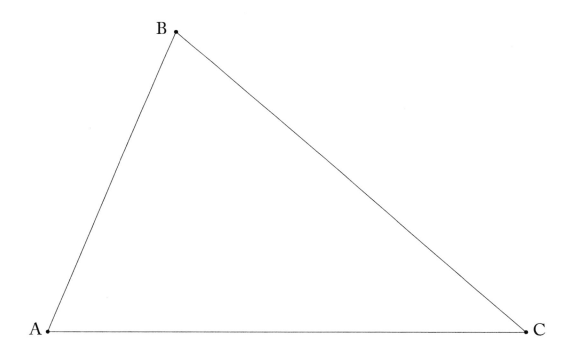

Lesson 3.5
Centers of a Triangle IV: Medians

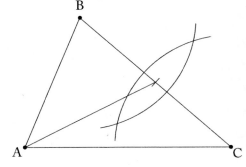

A **median** of a triangle is a segment that connects a vertex to the midpoint of the opposite side.

1. In ∆ABC below, construct the **midpoint** of side $\overline{BC}$. (To do this, construct its perpendicular bisector—but make it *very short*, just long enough to cross $\overline{BC}$ and locate its midpoint.)

2. Use the straightedge to connect the midpoint to its opposite vertex. This segment is a **median** (as shown at right).

3. Using the same method, construct the other two medians of ∆ABC.

4. The three medians should intersect in a single point. (If they don't, find your mistake and fix it!) Label this point the **centroid**.

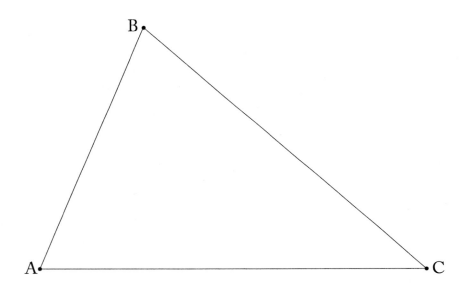

The centroid splits each median into two parts, one short and one long. How much longer is the long part? To answer this question, choose any one of the medians, and open your compass radius to the size of its short part. Exactly how many short parts will fit into the long part? _____

Extra Credit: Obtain a piece of cardboard, draw any triangle on it, locate its centroid, and cut out the triangle. It will balance at its centroid on the tip of a pin!

Lesson 3.6
The Nine-Point Circle

If you enjoyed constructing the orthocenter, circumcenter, and centroid, then you may enjoy the challenge of putting them into the same picture.

1. In ΔABC below, construct all three **altitudes**, and label the orthocenter, O.

2. Construct all three **perpendicular bisectors**, and label the circumcenter, Ci.

3. Construct all three **medians**, and label the centroid, Ce.

4. Draw the segment $\overline{OCi}$ connecting the orthocenter and the circumcenter. (If you have worked very carefully, the centroid, Ce, will lie on this segment.)

5. Open your compass radius to the length CiCe.

---

a. How many of these lengths will fit into the segment $\overline{OCe}$? _____

---

6. Construct the midpoint of the segment $\overline{OCi}$. Label it M.

7. Construct a circle with center M and passing through the midpoint of any side. This is called the **Nine-Point Circle**.

---

b. Find and list all nine interesting points that it passes through. (There are three types, each with three points.)

_____

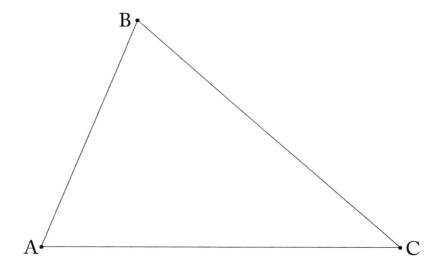

Chapter 4: Perpendiculars and Rectangles

Lesson 4.1
Erect a Perpendicular

In Lesson 3.1, you learned to drop a perpendicular from an external point to a given line. You used this method to construct the altitudes of triangles. It also is possible to erect a perpendicular from a point *on* a given line, like F on the segment below. We will use the fact that *two points equidistant from the endpoints of a segment determine its perpendicular bisector.* In the example to the right, F and Q are the two equidistant points.

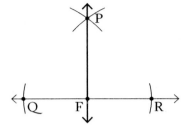

1. First, use your straightedge to make the segment below longer.

2. Using any convenient radius (not too short), construct two arcs with center F crossing the segment on opposite sides of the center. Label the crossing points, Q and R. (Note that F is equidistant from Q and R.)

3. Using any longer radius, construct an arc above F with center Q.

4. Using the same radius, construct an arc with center R above F.

5. Label the point where these two arcs cross, P. (Note that P is also equidistant from Q and R.)

6. Draw $\overleftrightarrow{PF}$. $\overleftrightarrow{PF}$ is the perpendicular bisector of $\overline{QR}$. F is called the **foot** of this perpendicular.

Can you imagine $\overleftrightarrow{PF}$ as the main diagonal of a kite?

•
_____
F

Lesson 4.2
Construct a Parallel Line I: Using a Perpendicular

Parallel lines never meet. Through the point P below, we can construct a line that is parallel to line *l*. We will use the theorem that *two lines perpendicular to the same line are parallel.*

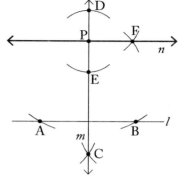

1. Drop a perpendicular from P to line *l*. (To do this, draw two arcs with center P that cross *l* at A and B. Draw two more arcs with centers A and B that intersect at C below the lines. Draw $\overrightarrow{PC}$.) Extend $\overrightarrow{PC}$ above P.

2. Erect a line through P perpendicular to $\overrightarrow{PC}$. (To do this, draw two arcs with center P that cross $\overrightarrow{PC}$ at D and E. Draw two arcs with centers D and E that intersect at F. Draw $\overrightarrow{PF}$.)

3. Lines *l* and $\overrightarrow{PF}$ are parallel, because they are both perpendicular to $\overrightarrow{PC}$.

. P

_____ *l*

Lesson 4.3
Construct a Rectangle When Given Two Sides I

A **rectangle** is a quadrilateral with four right angles. You can construct a rectangle by erecting perpendiculars. (You learned how to erect a perpendicular in Lesson 4.1.)

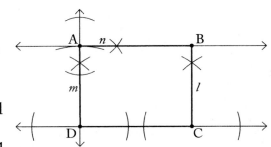

Build your rectangle on side $\overline{CD}$ below. Make the shorter sides the same length as $\overline{QP}$. The construction will look like the picture at right.

1. Erect a line through D perpendicular to $\overline{CD}$. Label the line, *m*.

2. Open your compass radius to the length QP. Make an arc with center D, above D. Label the point where the arc crosses line *m*, A.

3. Erect a line through A perpendicular to *m*. Label the line, *n*.

4. Erect a line through C perpendicular to $\overline{CD}$. Label the line, *l*.

5. Label the point where *l* crosses *n*, B. Then ABCD is a rectangle, because all of its sides are perpendicular.

Q

P

D   C

$\overline{AB}$ and $\overline{CD}$ are **opposite sides** of rectangle ABCD. $\overline{BC}$ and $\overline{DA}$ also are opposite sides.

In what two ways are opposite sides of a rectangle related to each other?

_____

_____

Lesson 4.4
Construct a Rectangle When Given Two Sides II

Opposite sides of a rectangle are equal in length. This property provides a quicker way to construct a rectangle. First construct one right angle, and then make all of the sides the correct lengths. Your construction will look like the drawing on the right.

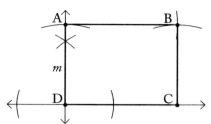

1. Erect a line through D perpendicular to $\overline{CD}$. Label the line, *m*.

2. Open your compass radius to the length QP. Make an arc with center D, above D. Label the point where the arc crosses line *m*, A.

3. Keeping the same radius QP, make an arc with center C, above C.

4. Change the radius to DC, and make an arc with center A, to the right of A.

5. Label the point where these arcs cross, B.

6. Draw $\overline{AB}$ and $\overline{BC}$. ABCD is a rectangle, because its opposite sides are equal and it has a right angle.

Q
•
│
│
│
│
│
│
•
P

•————————————————————————————————•
D   C

Now, draw the diagonals of rectangle ABCD.

In what two ways are the diagonals of a rectangle related to each other?

_____

_____

Lesson 4.5
Construct a Square When Given Its Side

A **square** is a special type of rectangle in which all four sides are the same length. In Lesson 2.5, you constructed a square given its *diagonal*. Now, use what you have learned about rectangles to construct a square given its *side*. Build your square on side $\overline{DC}$ below. Show all of the construction arcs you need—don't erase them!

a. Describe each step of your construction.

1. Erect a line through D perpendicular to $\overline{CD}$. Label the line, *m*.

2. _____

3. _____

4. _____

5. _____

6. _____

7. _____

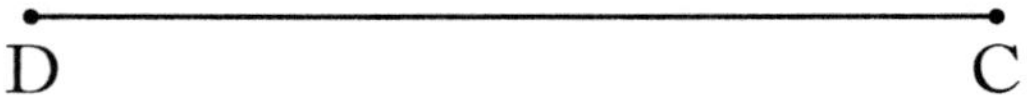

D●——●C

Draw the diagonals of square ABCD.

b. In what four ways are the diagonals of a square related to each other (or to the angles of the square)?

_____

_____

Chapter 5:
Parallels and Parallelograms

Lesson 5.1
Copy an Angle

To copy an angle means to construct an angle with the same measure but located somewhere else. You will copy angle A onto the line below. The finished construction will look like the drawing on the right.

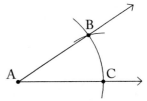

1. Open your compass to any convenient radius.

2. Draw an arc with center A that crosses both sides of angle A. Label the points where the arc crosses the sides of the angle, B and C, with B above C.

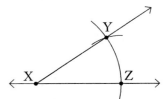

3. Keeping the same radius, draw an arc with center X. Make the arc about the same length as the arc you drew in step 2. Label the point where the arc crosses the working line, Z.

4. Draw a short arc with center C passing through B, so that the radius of the compass is the length BC.

5. Keeping the radius BC, draw an arc with center Z. Label the point where the two arcs cross, Y.

6. Draw $\overrightarrow{XY}$.

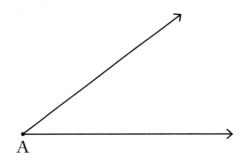

A

X

Angle YXZ is a copy of angle BAC. We also say that angle YXZ is **congruent** to angle BAC. In symbols, we write $\angle YXZ \cong \angle BAC$.

Lesson 5.2
Construct a Parallel Line II: Using an Oblique Line

This construction shows that you don't need perpendiculars to construct parallels. We will use an **oblique** line $\overleftrightarrow{PB}$. (An oblique line is neither perpendicular nor parallel to a given line.)

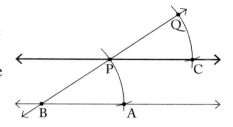

To construct a parallel line through P, you will copy the angle with vertex B to a corresponding position with vertex P. The construction will look like the picture at right.

1. Draw an arc with center B and passing through P. Label the point where the arc crosses the horizontal line, A.

2. Keeping the same radius, draw an arc with center P that crosses the oblique line above P and curves to the right. Label the point where the arc crosses the oblique line, Q.

3. Change the radius so you can draw an arc with center P that passes through A.

4. Keeping the radius PA, draw an arc with center Q that crosses the other arc with center P. Label the point where the arcs cross, C.

5. Draw $\overleftrightarrow{PC}$, which is parallel to the horizontal line. (Do you see that you have copied angle B?)

6. To see why these lines are parallel, observe that $\angle PBA$ is congruent to $\angle QPC$. *If corresponding angles are congruent, then lines are parallel.*

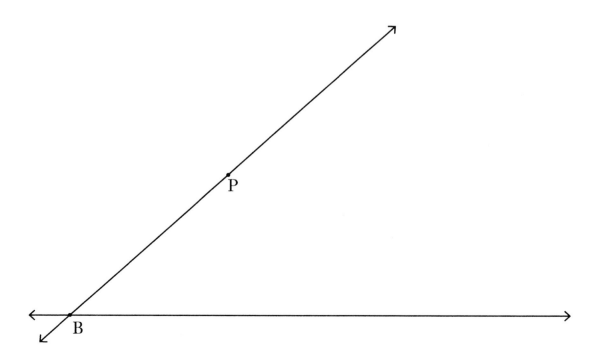

Lesson 5.3
Construct a Parallelogram I: Using the Definition

By definition, a **parallelogram** is a quadrilateral in which both pairs of opposite sides are parallel. Use point P and side $\overline{SR}$ below to construct a parallelogram. The construction will look like to the one on the right.

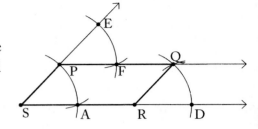

1. Draw ray $\overrightarrow{SP}$ (which includes side $\overline{SP}$). Also extend ray $\overrightarrow{SR}$ to the right.

2. Open your compass to the radius $\overline{SP}$. Draw an arc with center S and passing through P. Label the point where this arc crosses $\overrightarrow{SR}$, A.

3. Keeping the same radius, draw an arc with center P, about the same size. Label the point where this arc crosses $\overrightarrow{SP}$, E.

4. Keeping the same radius, draw an arc with center R, about the same size. Label the point where this arc crosses $\overrightarrow{SR}$, D.

5. Change your compass radius to PA. Draw an arc with center E. Label the point where this arc crosses the arc with center P, F. (Do you see that you are copying angle S?)

6. Draw the line $\overleftrightarrow{PF}$, which will be parallel to $\overline{SR}$, because *if corresponding angles are congruent, then lines are parallel.*

7. Keeping the radius PA, draw an arc with center D that crosses the arc with center R. If all has gone well, this arc will cross the parallel line at the same point. Label this point Q. Draw $\overline{RQ}$. (Do you see that ∠QRD is a copy of angle S?) Because corresponding angles are congruent, $\overline{RQ}$ is parallel to $\overline{SP}$.

8. Because both pairs of opposite sides are parallel, PQRS is a parallelogram by the definition.

$\bullet$ P

S $\bullet$————————————————————————$\bullet$ R

Lesson 5.4
Discerning Properties of Parallelograms

Look back at parallelogram PQRS you constructed in Lesson 5.3. Answer the following questions about it by circling the appropriate responses.

a. $\overline{PS}$ and $\overline{QR}$ are called **opposite sides**. $\overline{PQ}$ and $\overline{SR}$ also are opposite sides. Are these pairs of opposite sides parallel?

      Yes   No

b. Segments that have the same length are called **congruent**. Are opposite sides in parallelogram PQRS congruent?

      Yes   No

c. Do you think opposite sides of *any* parallelogram would be congruent? (*Hint*: Think about drawing the arc with center R in Step 4.)

      Yes   No

d. In PQRS, angles PSR and RQP are called **opposite angles**. Angles QPS and SRQ are also opposite angles. Are opposite angles congruent?

      Yes   No

e. Do you think opposite angles of *any* parallelogram would be congruent?

      Yes   No

f. Angles PSR and QRS and are called **consecutive angles**. What relationship do consecutive angles have to each other? (*Hint:* Remember that $\angle PSR \cong \angle QRD$.)

    i. Consecutive angles are congruent.
    ii. Consecutive angles are supplementary (their sum is 180°).
    iii. Consecutive angles are complementary (their sum is 90°).

Now, turn back to your construction in Lesson 5.3 and draw the diagonals $\overline{SQ}$ and $\overline{PR}$. Answer the following questions by circling the appropriate responses.

g. Are the diagonals of PQRS congruent?

      Yes   No

h. Are the diagonals of PQRS perpendicular to each other?

      Yes   No

i. Do the diagonals of PQRS bisect its angles?

      Yes   No

j. Do the diagonals of PQRS bisect each other?

      Yes   No

Lesson 5.5
Construct a Parallelogram II: An Easier Way

One geometry theorem states that, *if two sides of a quadrilateral are both parallel and congruent, then it is a parallelogram.* This fact implies an easier way to construct a parallelogram.

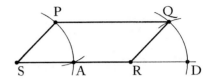

Use point P and side $\overline{SR}$ below. You will construct $\overline{RQ}$ both parallel and congruent to $\overline{SP}$.

1. Draw ray $\overrightarrow{SR}$ (which includes side $\overline{SR}$). Draw ray $\overrightarrow{SP}$.

2. Draw an arc with radius SP and center S. Label the point where this arc crosses $\overline{SR}$, A.

3. Keeping the same radius, draw an arc with center R to the right of R. Label the point where this arc crosses $\overline{SR}$, D.

4. Open your compass radius to PA. Draw an arc with center D that crosses the arc with center R. Label the point where these arcs cross, Q. Draw $\overline{RQ}$ and $\overline{PQ}$.

5. Because $\overline{PS}$ is parallel and congruent to $\overline{QR}$, PQRS is a parallelogram.

• P

•————————————————————————————•
S   R

Lesson 5.6
Construct a Parallelogram III: The Easiest Way

Yet another geometry theorem states that, *if both pairs of opposite sides of a quadrilateral are congruent, then it is a parallelogram.* Show how to use this theorem to construct parallelogram PQRS below. Describe each step of your construction. (Hint: You only need to draw two arcs to locate point Q.)

1. _____

2. _____

3. _____

4. _____

$\bullet$
P

$\bullet$ _____ $\bullet$
S   R

Chapter 6:
Constructing Triangles

Lesson 6.1
Construct a Triangle Given SSS

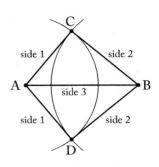

Suppose you are given three lengths. Can you construct a triangle using those lengths as its three sides? In other words, given **Side-Side-Side (SSS)**, can you construct a triangle? Could you construct two different triangles using the same three sides? If three given sides can be used to construct one and only one triangle, then we will say that **SSS determines a triangle**. But, does it matter how long the sides are?

Below are three side lengths, side 1, side 2, and side 3. We will build triangles above and below side 3. The finished construction will look like the picture at right.

1. Open your compass radius to be the length of side 1.

2. Keeping that radius, draw a big arc—half of a circle—with center A and radius side 1. The arc should cross $\overline{AB}$.

3. Open your compass radius to be the length of side 2.

4. Draw a big arc with center B and radius side 2.

5. Label the points where the two arcs cross, C and D.

6. Draw $\overline{AC}$ and $\overline{BC}$, and label them side 1 and side 2.

7. Draw $\overline{AD}$ and $\overline{BD}$, and also label them side 1 and side 2.

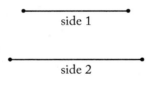

side 1

side 2

A   side 3   B

a. Using your imagination, how could you move ΔABC to fit on top of ΔABD?

_____

_____

b. Do ΔABC and ΔABD have the same size and shape? _____

c. In this case, does SSS determine a triangle? _____

8. Suppose we make side 3 a little longer. Use the SSS method to construct ΔABE with these three side lengths. Make just one triangle, either above or below $\overline{AB}$.

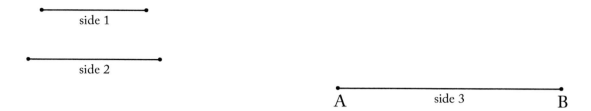

side 1

side 2

A   side 3   B

---

d. For this obtuse triangle, does SSS determine a triangle? _____

---

9. Now let's make side 3 even longer. Try to construct a triangle with these three side lengths:

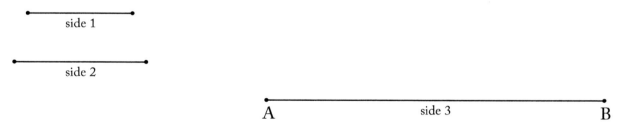

side 1

side 2

A   side 3   B

---

e. What went wrong?

_____

_____

f. In order to be able to construct a triangle, how must the length of side 3 be related to the lengths of the two shorter sides?

_____

_____

g. Given three sides that fit this restriction, will SSS determine a triangle? _____

Lesson 6.2
Using SSS to Copy a Triangle Into Kites or Parallelograms

Follow these directions to create a copy of ΔPQR flipped over side $\overline{PR}$.
1. Draw an arc with center P and radius PQ on the left side of ΔPQR.
2. Draw an arc with center R and radius RQ on the left side of ΔPQR.
3. Label the point where the arcs intersect, S.
4. Draw segments $\overline{PS}$ and $\overline{RS}$.

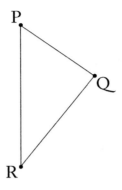

a. What special type of quadrilateral is PQRS? _____

Construct three copies of the triangle below, flipping it over each side. You will draw six arcs. Each side is the radius of two arcs, one centered at each endpoint. The finished construction should look like the picture at right.

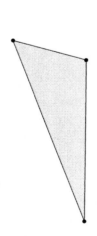

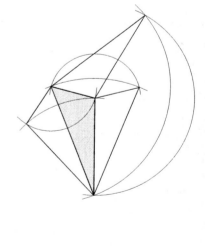

b. How many kites are in your construction? _____

Follow the directions below to create a copy of ΔPQR that has been rotated around the midpoint of side $\overline{PR}$.

1. Use radius QR to draw an arc with center P (!) on the left side of ΔPQR.

2. Switch to radius QP to draw an arc with center R (!) on the left side of ΔPQR.

3. Label the point where the arcs intersect, T.

4. Draw segments $\overline{PT}$ and $\overline{RT}$.

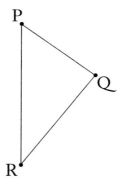

c. What special type of quadrilateral is PQRT? _____

Construct three copies of the triangle below, rotating it around the midpoint of each side. You will draw three circles. Each side is the radius of one circle with its center being the opposite vertex. The finished construction should look like the picture at right.

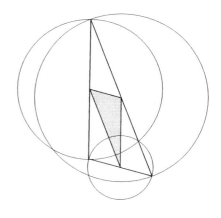

d. How many parallelograms are in your construction? _____

Lesson 6.2, Continued

Reconsider your construction as one large white triangle with a small grey triangle inside. Each side of the grey triangle is called a **midsegment** of the large white triangle, because each side of the grey triangle connects the midpoints of two sides of the white triangle.

> e. How does the length of each midsegment compare with the length of the side that it is parallel to?
>
> _____
>
> f. How does the area of the inner triangle compare with the area of the outer triangle?
>
> _____

Again reconsider your construction. The three circles shown in the picture intersect in three other points that were not used to form the parallelograms. Redraw those three circles below. Connect one of these other intersection points to the two nearest vertices of the grey triangle.

> g. What kind of special quadrilateral is formed? _____

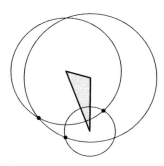

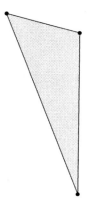

Lesson 6.3
Using SSS to Copy an Angle

This lesson verifies the method of Lesson 5.1. To copy an angle means to construct an angle with the same measure but located somewhere else. You will copy angle A onto the line below. The finished construction will look like the one on the right.

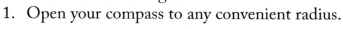

1. Open your compass to any convenient radius.

2. Draw an arc with center A that crosses both sides of angle A. Label the points where the arc crosses the sides of the angle, B and C, with B above C.

3. Keeping the same radius, draw an arc with center X. Make the arc about the same length as the arc you drew in step 2. Label the point where the arc crosses the working line, Z.

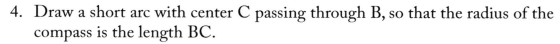

4. Draw a short arc with center C passing through B, so that the radius of the compass is the length BC.

5. Keeping the radius BC, draw an arc with center Z. Label the point where the two arcs cross, Y.

6. Draw $\overrightarrow{XY}$.

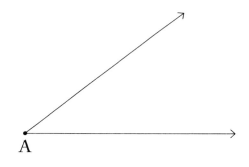

How can we be sure that angle YXZ is a copy of angle BAC? Because SSS determines a triangle, △YXZ and △BAC must have the same size and shape. Hence corresponding angles must have the same measure, so ∠YXZ ≅ ∠BAC.

Lesson 6.4
Construct a Triangle Given ASA

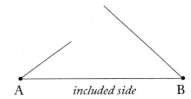

included side

The picture at left shows another way to think about constructing a triangle. Given a side and the two angles that fit on either end, can you construct one and only one triangle? In other words, does **Angle-Side-Angle (ASA)** determine a triangle? (The given side is "included" because it is a part of each angle.)

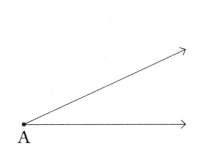

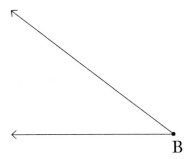

You will fit copies of angles A and B onto each endpoint of side $\overline{AB}$ below. The construction will look like the picture at right.

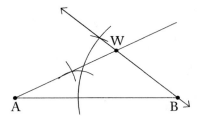

1. Copy angle A onto the left endpoint of $\overline{AB}$. (Use the method found in Lesson 6.3.)

2. Copy angle B onto the right endpoint of $\overline{AB}$.

3. Label the point where the rays cross, W. You have created Δ ABW.

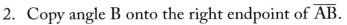

4. Here is an obtuse angle C that replaces angle A. Copy angle B onto the right endpoint of $\overline{CB}$ below to create ΔCBV.

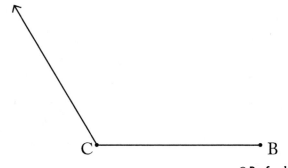

5. Here is a copy of angle C from the previous page, but a different angle B. Copy this angle B onto the right endpoint of $\overline{CB}$.

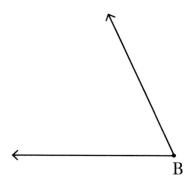

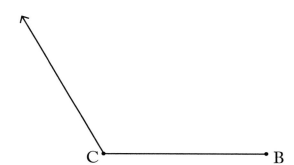

a. Why can't you construct ΔCBV in this case?

_____

_____

b. Does the length of the given side $\overline{CB}$ make any difference? _____

c. If the two given angles can belong to the same triangle, then their sum must be smaller than what number? _____

d. Given two angles that fit the restriction in question C, and the side included between them, will ASA determine a triangle? _____

Lesson 6.5
Construct a Triangle Given SAS

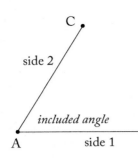

The picture at left indicates yet another possible way to construct a triangle. Suppose you are given two sides and the angle included between them. Can you construct one and only one triangle? In other words, does **Side-Angle-Side (SAS)** determine a triangle? Your finished construction will look like the picture at right.

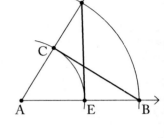

1. Copy side 1 onto the horizontal side of angle A; label the intersection point B.

2. Copy side 2 onto the oblique side of angle A; label the intersection point C.

3. Draw $\overline{BC}$.

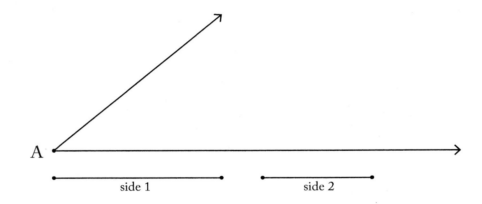

4. Now copy side 1 onto the *oblique* side of ∠A; label the intersection point D.

5. Copy side 2 onto the *horizontal* side of ∠A; label the intersection point E.

6. Draw $\overline{DE}$.

a. Does △ABC have the same size and shape as △ADE? _____

7. Now copy side 1 and side 2 onto this obtuse angle to form a triangle.

b. Does SAS determine a triangle even if the angle is obtuse? _____

c. Would it matter if the sides were longer or shorter? _____

d. Does SAS always determine a triangle? _____

Lesson 6.6
When Does SSA Determine a Triangle

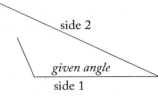

side 2

given angle

side 1

Suppose you are given an angle, a side adjacent to the angle (side 1), and a side opposite the angle (side 2). Does **Side-Side-Angle (SSA)** determine a triangle? The answer depends on the type of angle and on the relative lengths of the two sides. We investigate eight cases, first with an obtuse angle, then with a right angle, then with an acute angle.

Case I. The angle is obtuse, and side 2 is greater than side 1.
   1. Open your compass to the radius side 2, and make an arc with center B.

   2. Label the point where the arc crosses the oblique side of angle A, C.

   3. Draw $\overline{BC}$. Label it side 2.

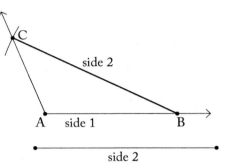

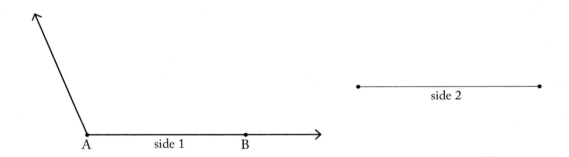

a. Did SSA determine a triangle in this case? _____

b. If side 2 were longer, would SSA determine a triangle? _____

Case II. The angle is obtuse, and side 2 is less than (or equal to) side 1.
   4. Open your compass to the radius side 2, and make an arc with center B.

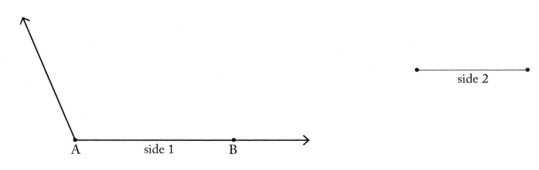

> c. How could you change the length of side 2 to be able to construct a triangle?
>
> _____
>
> d. Why would SsA be a good way to describe the construction method you investigated in Case I and Case II? (In your answer, refer to side 2 as "the side opposite the angle" and refer to side 1 as "the side adjacent to the angle.")
>
> _____

Case III. The angle is a right angle.
   5. Choose any length for side 2 greater than side 1, and construct a triangle.
   6. Choose any length for side 2 less than side 1, and try to construct a triangle.

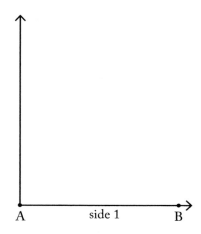

A   side 1   B

> e. If side 2 > side 1 and the angle is a right angle, does SsA determine a triangle?
>
> _____
>
> f. Let sSA mean side 2 < side 1. Would sSA ever determine a triangle when the angle is an obtuse or a right angle?
>
> _____
>
> g. Let ssA mean side 2 = side 1. Would ssA ever determine a triangle when the angle is an obtuse or a right angle?
>
> _____

Case IV. The angle is acute and side 2 is greater than side 1.

    7. Make an arc with center B and radius side 2.

    8. Label the point where this arc crosses the oblique side of angle A, C.

    9. Draw side $\overline{BC}$.

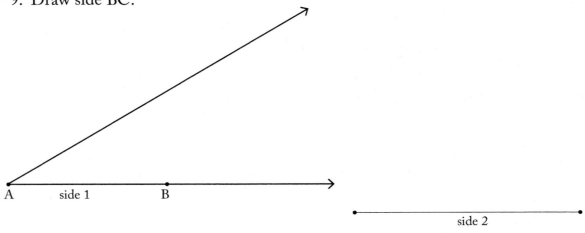

    h. Would anyone else get the same triangle you did? _____

  10. Open your compass to any other length of side 2 that is greater than side 1. Try to construct a triangle following steps 7–9.

    i. If the angle is acute and side 2 > side 1, does SsA determine a triangle? _____

Case V. The angle is acute, and side 2 is equal to side 1.

  11. Open your compass so its radius is the same as side 2.

  12. Make an arc with center B and radius side 2. Label the point where this arc crosses the oblique side of angle A, C.

  13. Draw side $\overline{BC}$.

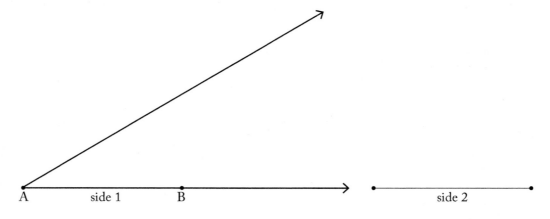

    j. If the angle is acute, does ssA determine a triangle? _____

Case VI. The angle is acute, and side 2 is somewhat shorter than side 1.

14. Open your compass so its radius is the same as side 2.

15. Make an arc with center B and radius side 2.

16. Label the two (!) points where this arc crosses the oblique side of angle A, C and D.

17. Draw sides $\overline{BC}$ and $\overline{BD}$.

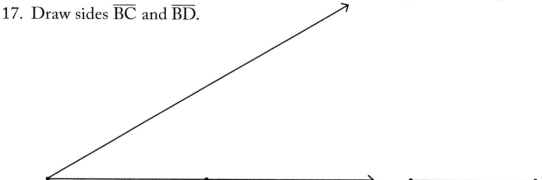

k. How many triangles have you drawn that use angle A, side 1, and this side 2?

_____

l. Does sSA determine one and only one triangle in this case? _____

18. Change your radius to be slightly smaller than side 2, and repeat steps 15–17. Change your radius again to be slightly smaller, and repeat steps 15–17.

m. Can you find just the right radius so that points C and D are in the same place?

_____

Case VII. Side 2 is just short enough to reach the oblique side of angle A.

19. Open your compass so its radius is the same as given side 2, which was carefully chosen to be just the right size.

20. Make an arc with center B and radius side 2.

21. This arc should touch the oblique side of angle A in just one point; label that point C.

22. Draw side $\overline{BC}$.

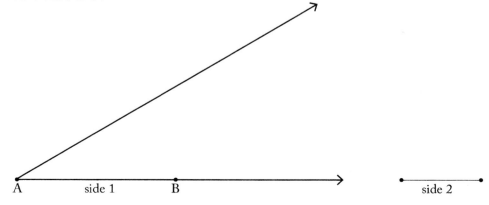

    n. What kind of angle is angle C? _____

    o. Does sSA determine a triangle in this special case? _____

Case VIII. Side 2 is too short to reach the oblique side of angle A.

  23. Open your compass so its radius is the same as side 2.

  24. Make an arc with center B and radius side 2.

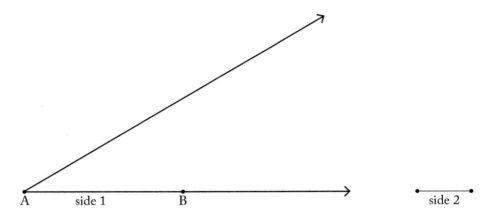

    p. Does the arc cross the oblique side of angle A? _____

    q. Does sSA determine a triangle in this case? _____

Summary of Cases

    r. These are the three conditions under which SSA determines a triangle:

       i. If **opposite side > adjacent side,** for what kinds of given angles does **SsA** determine a triangle? (*Circle all that apply.*)   obtuse   right   acute

      ii. If **opposite side = adjacent side,** for what kind of given angle does **ssA** determine a triangle? (*Circle one.*)   obtuse   right   acute

    iii. If **opposite side < adjacent side,** for what kind of given angle *might* **sSA** determine a triangle? (*Circle one.*)   obtuse   right   acute

    iv. If sSA does determine a triangle in condition iii, what type of triangle must it be?

    _____

Chapter 7:
The Infinitesimal
and the Golden Ratio

Lesson 7.1
Construct a Midsegment and Discern Its Properties

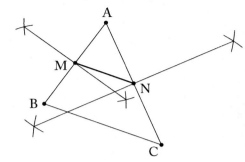

In earlier lessons, you constructed the midpoints of the sides of a triangle. In this lesson, you will connect two of those midpoints with a segment—the **midsegment**—and discern its properties.

1. In the space below, locate any three noncollinear points A, B, and C wherever you choose. Connect them to be the vertices of △ABC.

2. Use the perpendicular bisector construction (described in Lesson 2.4) to find the midpoints of $\overline{AB}$ and $\overline{AC}$. Label them M and N.

3. Draw $\overline{MN}$.

Find two interesting relationships between $\overline{MN}$ and $\overline{BC}$.

_____

_____

Lesson 7.2
Join the Midpoints of Any Quadrilateral

The midpoints of the sides of any quadrilateral have an interesting property. Construct them, and figure out what property they have.

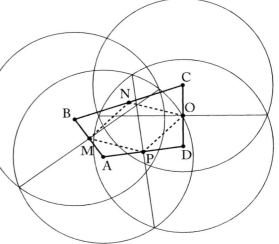

1. In the space below, locate any four noncollinear points A, B, C, and D.

2. Connect the points to form quadrilateral ABCD, as shown in the picture.

3. Choose any radius longer than half the longest side. Draw two circles, with centers A and B.

4. Connect the intersection points of circles A and B to find the midpoint, M.

5. Keeping the same radius, draw the circle with center C. Connect the intersection points of circles B and C to find the midpoint, N.

6. Keeping the same radius, draw the circle with center D. Connect the intersection points of circles C and D to find the midpoint, O.

7. Connect the intersection points of circles D and A to find the midpoint, P.

8. Connect the midpoints to form quadrilateral MNOP.

a. What special type of quadrilateral is MNOP? _____

To verify this conjecture, draw $\overline{AC}$ and answer these questions:
  b. Which segment is the midsegment of $\triangle ABC$? _____
  c. Which segment is the midsegment of $\triangle ADC$? _____
  d. Why is $\overline{MN}$ parallel to $\overline{OP}$?

_____

_____

  e. Why are $\overline{MN}$ and $\overline{OP}$ the same length?

_____

_____

  f. Why is MNOP the special type of quadrilateral you declared it to be?

_____

_____

Lesson 7.3
Join the Midpoints of a Rectangle and Peer Into the Infinitesimal

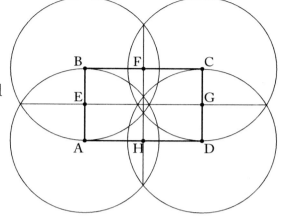

1. Open your compass radius to the length of $\overline{AB}$. Construct circles with centers A, B, C, and D.

2. Connect appropriate intersections of these circles to locate the midpoints of rectangle ABCD. Label them E, F, G, and H. (These are shown in the example figure to the right.)

3. Connect these midpoints to form quadrilateral EFGH.

4. Draw diagonals $\overline{BD}$ and $\overline{AC}$.

5. Diagonals $\overline{BD}$ and $\overline{AC}$ intersect the sides of EFGH in midpoints I, J, K, and L. Label these midpoints. Connect them to form quadrilateral IJKL.

6. Diagonals $\overline{EG}$ and $\overline{FH}$ intersect the sides of IJKL in their midpoints; connect these midpoints to form another quadrilateral.

7. Continue connecting midpoints to get smaller and smaller quadrilaterals. In theory, you could go on forever.

   a. What special type of quadrilateral is EFGH? _____

   b. What special type of quadrilateral is IJKL? _____

Lesson 7.4
Fill a Golden Rectangle to the Infinitesimal

Some rectangles are long and thin, and others are square. Since the time of the ancient Greeks, many people have felt that the most perfectly proportioned rectangle is the golden rectangle. The pillars of the Parthenon, the Cathedral of Notre Dame, and the United Nations Building in New York all utilize the golden rectangle in their design.

A **golden rectangle** can be divided into a square and another, smaller golden rectangle.

1. Open your compass radius to length GO. Swing an arc with center G from O across $\overline{GD}$. Label the point where the arc crosses $\overline{GD}$, E.

2. Keeping the same radius, draw an arc with center O across $\overline{OL}$. Label the intersection point, N.

3. Connect $\overline{EN}$ to form square GONE and another golden rectangle, LDEN.

4. Repeat this procedure to divide each golden rectangle into a square and a smaller golden rectangle, as far as you can. In theory, you could go on forever.

Lesson 7.5
Calculate the Golden Ratio

(For students who can use the quadratic formula.)

Many of the rectangles we use every day are close to being golden. File cards are 3 × 5, 4 × 6, or 5 × 8, and legal-size paper is 8½ × 14; these shapes are very close to being golden rectangles. Leonardo da Vinci showed that many of the proportions of the human body and face are based on the golden rectangle, and he used golden rectangles to place key features in his painting, *Mona Lisa*.

How do you determine the shape of the golden rectangle? The shape of any rectangle is determined by the ratio of its length to its width. For a square, this ratio is 1. For other rectangles, this ratio could be any number from 1 to infinity.

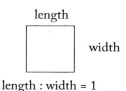

length : width = 1

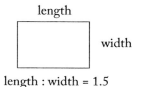

length : width = 1.5

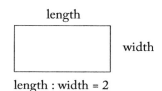

length : width = 2

The ratio of length to width of a golden rectangle is called the **golden ratio**.

a. Compare the golden rectangle to the right to the rectangles shown above. What number would you guess to be close to the golden ratio?

_____

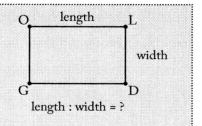

length : width = ?

To calculate the golden ratio exactly, consider golden rectangle GOLD, which has length GD = x and width LD = 1. Hence $\frac{x}{1}$ must be the golden ratio. We can divide GOLD into the 1 × 1 square GONE and the smaller golden rectangle LDEN, which has length 1 and width $x - 1$. Hence $\frac{1}{x-1}$ must also be the golden ratio. Thus we get the equation $\frac{x}{1} = \frac{1}{x-1}$.

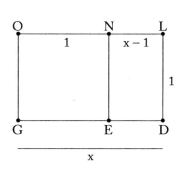

b. Show how to use the quadratic formula to solve the above equation and find the exact form for the golden ratio (which is often called ϕ, *phi*).

Lesson 7.6
Construct a Golden Rectangle

As you calculated in Lesson 7.5, the golden ratio is $\phi = \frac{1+\sqrt{5}}{2}$.
Note that this expression takes the square root of the integer
5, adds 1, and then divides by 2. All of these operations
can be shown to be **constructible**. (We will investigate
construction arithmetic in Chapter 10.) Given segment
$\overline{GO}$ below that has length 1, it is possible to construct a
perpendicular segment $\overline{OL}$ that has length $\phi = \frac{1+\sqrt{5}}{2}$.

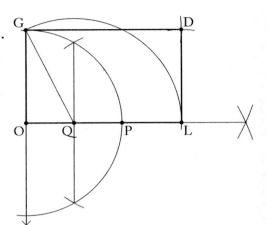

1. Extend ray $\overrightarrow{GO}$.

2. Erect a perpendicular to $\overline{GO}$ through O.

3. Locate point P on that perpendicular such that $OP = OG$.

4. Find the midpoint of $\overline{OP}$; label it Q. Draw $\overline{GQ}$.

5. Draw an arc with center Q and radius QG; label the point where the arc crosses
   the perpendicular, L. Point L is the third corner of the golden rectangle.

6. Draw an arc with radius OG and center L; draw an arc with radius OL and center
   G; label the intersection of these arcs D. D is the fourth corner of the rectangle.

7. Connect golden rectangle GOLD.

Why does this construction work? Because $GO = 1$, $OQ = \frac{1}{2}$, and, by the
Pythagorean Theorem, $GQ = \frac{\sqrt{5}}{2}$; therefore, $OL = \frac{1+\sqrt{5}}{2}$.

G.

O.

Lesson 7.7
Construct a Regular Pentagon

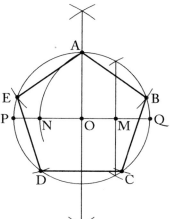

As you have worked through these lessons, you have constructed an equilateral triangle, a square, and a regular hexagon, octagon, and dodecagon. But you have not yet constructed a **regular pentagon** that has five equal sides and five equal angles. The construction is tricky, but fun. Be precise and use a sharp pencil!

1. Construct the perpendicular bisector of $\overline{PQ}$ below. Label the midpoint O.

2. Draw the circle with center O and passing through P and Q.

3. Label the point where the circle crosses the perpendicular above O, A.

4. Construct the midpoint of $\overline{OQ}$; label it M. (Hint: Don't change the radius; draw arcs with center Q.)

5. Draw an arc with center M and radius MA. Label the point where the arc crosses $\overline{PQ}$, N.

6. Open your compass radius to the length AN. This is a side of your pentagon. Draw two arcs with center A that cross circle O. Label the left intersection E and the right one B.

7. Keeping the same radius, draw an arc with center B across the circle; label the intersection point C. Draw another arc with center E across the circle; label the intersection point D.

8. Draw the five sides of the regular pentagon ABCDE.

P._____.Q

Chapter 8:
Similar Triangles

Lesson 8.1
Testing Whether Angles Are Congruent

In an earlier lesson, you learned to copy an angle, thus *creating* congruent angles. A variation on this method will enable you to test whether two *existing* angles are congruent.

Follow the steps to find which of the angles below, W, X, Y, or Z, is congruent to angle V. The sample diagram shows what to do for angle W; follow a similar process for angles X, Y, and Z.

1. Open your compass to any convenient radius. Draw an arc with center V that crosses the sides of angle V in two points; label these points P and Q.

2. Keeping the same radius, draw similar arcs with centers W, X, Y, and Z, crossing the sides of those angles.

3. Label one point where the arc crosses angle W, P1.

4. Label points where the arcs cross angles X, Y, and Z, P2, P3, and P4.

5. Adjust the radius of your compass so that you can draw an arc with center P that passes exactly through point Q.

6. Keeping the radius PQ, draw an arc with center P1 that crosses the other arc.

7. Repeat step 4 for points P2, P3, and P4.

a. For angle W, where do the two arcs cross: inside, outside, or on the side of the angle?

_____

b. For an angle to be congruent to angle V, where should the arcs cross: inside, outside, or on the side of the angle?

_____

c. Which angle is congruent to angle V? _____

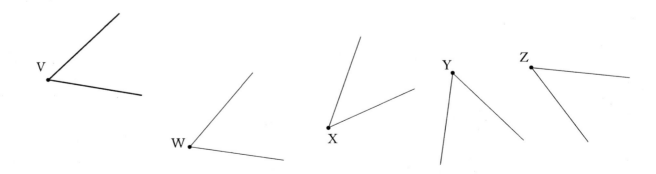

Lesson 8.2
AA Similarity

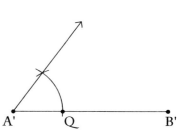

Suppose you are given a triangle. By copying two of its angles, you can construct a **similar** triangle that has the same shape, but may be a different size.

1. Use the method found in Lesson 5.1 to copy angle A onto $\overline{A'B'}$, with vertex A'. The steps are shown in the sample diagram.

2. Using the same procedure on the other end, copy angle B onto $\overline{B'A'}$. (This is not shown.)

3. Label the point where the two rays cross, C'.

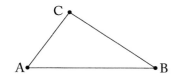

A' •——• B'

---

a. Is angle C congruent to angle C'? (Use the method of Lesson 8.1 to be sure.)

_____

b. Use your compass to find the ratio $\dfrac{A'B'}{AB}$. (Hint: How many copies of $\overline{AB}$ will fit onto $\overline{A'B'}$?)

_____

c. Use your compass to find the ratios $\dfrac{A'C'}{AC}$ and $\dfrac{B'C'}{BC}$.

_____

Because these three ratios are all the same, we say that corresponding sides of $\triangle A'B'C'$ and $\triangle ABC$ are **proportional**. We say that $\triangle ABC$ is similar to $\triangle A'B'C'$, and we write $\triangle ABC \sim \triangle A'B'C'$. As a formal definition, two triangles are **similar** whenever their corresponding angles are congruent and their corresponding sides are proportional.

This lesson demonstrates a quick way to ensure that triangles are similar, called **AA Similarity**: *If two triangles have two pairs of corresponding angles that are congruent, then the triangles are similar.*

Lesson 8.3
Expanding and Contracting Triangles

In this lesson, you will make triangle ABC expand and contract. The technical term for expanding is **dilation**, and the point P below is called the **center of dilation**.

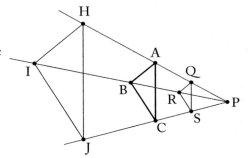

1. Draw rays $\overrightarrow{PA}$, $\overrightarrow{PB}$, and $\overrightarrow{PC}$.

2. Construct the midpoints of $\overline{PA}$, $\overline{PB}$, and $\overline{PC}$; label them Q, R, and S. (Hint: You can construct all three midpoints without changing your compass radius.)

3. Connect the sides of $\triangle QRS$.

4. Locate H on $\overrightarrow{PA}$ such that PA = AH. Locate I on $\overrightarrow{PB}$ such that PB = BI, and locate J on $\overrightarrow{PC}$ such that PC = CJ.

5. Connect the sides of $\triangle HIJ$.

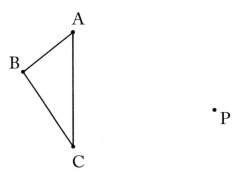

a. Find the ratios $\dfrac{QR}{AB}$, $\dfrac{RS}{BC}$, and $\dfrac{QS}{AC}$. _____

b. Find the ratios $\dfrac{HI}{AB}$, $\dfrac{IJ}{BC}$, and $\dfrac{HJ}{AC}$. _____

c. Test whether angle BAC is congruent to angle IHJ. Also test any other pair of corresponding angles. Are they congruent?

_____

d. Are the three triangles similar? _____

This lesson demonstrates another quick way to ensure that triangles are similar, called **SSS Similarity**: *If all three corresponding sides of two triangles are proportional, then the triangles are similar.*

Lesson 8.4
Splitting the Sides of a Triangle

When you split the sides of a triangle with a line parallel to its base, you get similar triangles. Your construction will look like the picture to the right.

1. On △ABC below, locate point P anywhere you chose on side $\overline{AB}$.
2. Construct an arc with radius BC and center P, to the right of point C.
3. Construct an arc with radius BP and center C.
4. Label the point where the two arcs cross, R.
5. Draw $\overline{PR}$ and $\overline{CR}$.
6. Label the point where $\overline{PR}$ intersects $\overline{AC}$, Q.

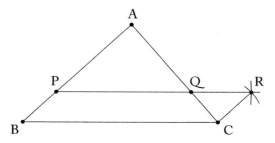

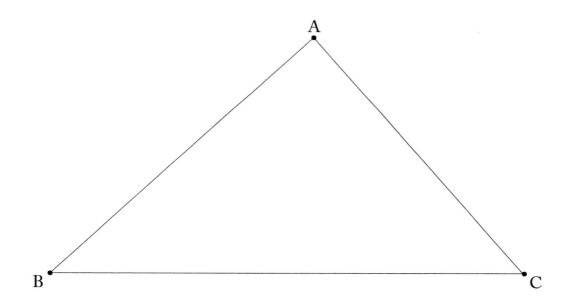

a. How does your construction ensure that PRCB is a parallelogram?

_____

_____

b. Which property of parallel lines ensures that ∠ABC ≅ ∠APQ and ∠ACB ≅ ∠AQP?

_____

_____

c. In your construction, mark three congruent angles with single arcs and three other congruent angles with double arcs.

d. Which two triangles are similar to $\triangle ABC$? Write the letters in order so that the first letter is congruent to A, the second letter is congruent to B, and the third letter is congruent to C. Also, tell how you know the triangles are similar.

$\triangle ABC \sim \triangle$ _____ $\sim \triangle$ _____

because of_____

e. Fill in the numerators to show which ratios are equal:

$$\frac{\quad}{AB} = \frac{\quad}{AC} = \frac{\quad}{BC} \quad \text{and} \quad \frac{\quad}{AB} = \frac{\quad}{AC} = \frac{\quad}{BC}.$$

Lesson 8.5
Similarity in a Right Triangle

Consider $\triangle ABC$ below, which has right angle C, acute angle A marked with a single arc, and acute angle B marked with a double arc. Imagine a point D on side $\overline{AB}$, and imagine segment $\overline{CD}$ that divides $\triangle ABC$ into two triangles, $\triangle I$ and $\triangle II$. Where should point D be located so that these two triangles are similar to each other and similar to $\triangle ABC$?

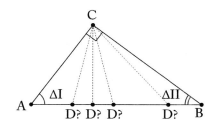

a. Tell how to construct point D, then construct and label D on $\triangle ABC$ below.

_____

_____

b.　i. In your construction, write "$\triangle I$" inside $\triangle ACD$ and "$\triangle II$" inside $\triangle CBD$.

　　ii. Find another angle congruent to $\angle A$, and mark it with a single arc.

　　iii. Find another angle congruent to $\angle B$, and mark it with a double arc.

c. Which triangles are similar? (Hint: Write the letters in the order "single arc, double arc, right angle.")

　　$\triangle ABC \sim \triangle$_____ $\sim \triangle$_____.

d. How do you know those triangles are similar? _____

e. Fill in the denominators to show which ratios are equal.

(Hint: Think $\dfrac{\text{short side } \triangle I}{\text{short side } \triangle II} = \dfrac{\text{medium side } \triangle I}{\text{medium side } \triangle II}$.)　　$\dfrac{AD}{\rule{1.5cm}{0.4pt}} = \dfrac{CD}{\rule{1.5cm}{0.4pt}}$.

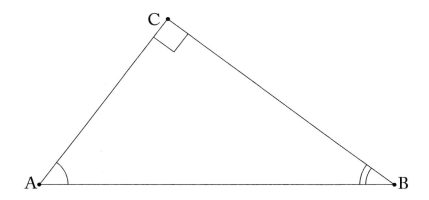

Lesson 8.6
Similarity in Design

Use similar triangles to construct the evergreen tree shown at right.
(Add the trunk freehand.)

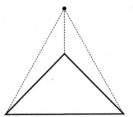

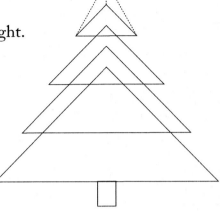

Chapter 9:
Circles and Tangents

Lesson 9.1
Angles Inscribed in a Semicircle

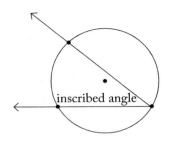

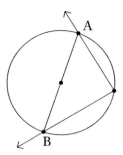

An angle is **inscribed** in a circle if its vertex lies on that circle and each of its sides crosses that circle in another place as well. An angle is **inscribed in a semicircle** if its sides cross through endpoints of a diameter.

1. Choose and label any point A on circle O below. Draw the diameter with endpoint A through O. Label the other endpoint B.

2. Pick any other point C on the circle. Draw $\overline{AC}$ and $\overline{BC}$.

   a. What special kind of angle do you suppose angle C is? _____

3. Pick another point D on the circle. Draw $\overline{AD}$ and $\overline{BD}$.

   b. What special kind of angle do you suppose angle D is? _____

   c. What do you suppose is true about *any* angle inscribed in a semicircle?

   _____

   _____

•O

Name_____   Date_____

Lesson 9.2:
Construct a Rectangle (Given Its Diagonal and One Side)

In an earlier lesson, you constructed a rectangle given the lengths of its sides. Now, figure out how to construct a rectangle ABCD using $\overline{AC}$ below as its diagonal. (Hint: Use the method of the previous lesson to construct the right angles at B and at D.)

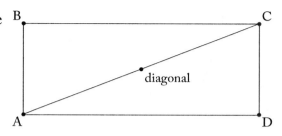

Write the steps of your construction method below.

1. _____

2. _____

3. _____

4. _____

5. _____

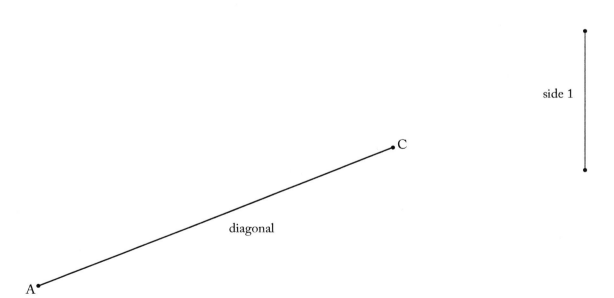

Lesson 9.3
Construct a Tangent to a Circle

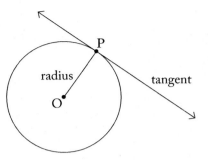

A **tangent** to a circle is a line that touches the circle in exactly one point, which is called the **point of tangency**. A theorem from geometry states that *a tangent to a circle is perpendicular to the radius drawn to the point of tangency.*

   The circle below has center O and passes through point P. Figure out how to construct the line through P that is tangent to circle O. You can't just guess! (Hint: Erect a perpendicular at P.)

Write the steps of your construction below.

1. _____

2. _____

3. _____

4. _____

5. _____

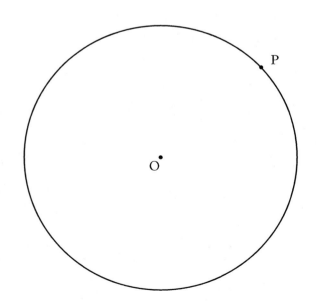

Lesson 9.4
Construct a Tangent to a Circle From an External Point

What if the point P is not on the circle? Can you still construct a line through P that is tangent to the circle? It's not acceptable to slide your straightedge around and guess. You have to *construct* the tangent, and you need *two* points to determine a line. But, how do you find the point of tangency before you draw the tangent?

You may need to ponder this question for a while. Here are some hints: Can you find a rectangle hiding in this picture? How could you construct that rectangle? Have you solved a similar problem before?

Construct the tangent from P to circle O below. Write the steps of your construction method. Show all the arcs you need.

1. _____

2. _____

3. _____

4. _____

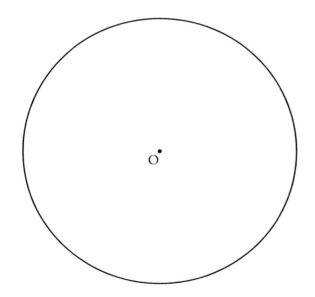

Lesson 9.5
Construct a Common External Tangent to Two Circles

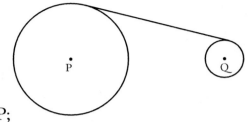

In this lesson, you will construct a segment that is tangent to each of two circles. (This tangent could be the path that a belt follows between two pulleys.) Our method will be to construct: first, the *difference* between the radii of the two circles; second, a circle with that radius concentric to circle P; third, tangent $\overline{EQ}$; and fourth, rectangle EQGF. $\overline{FG}$ will be the desired external tangent.

1. Draw $\overrightarrow{PQ}$; label the point where $\overrightarrow{PQ}$ crosses circle P, A. Label the point where $\overrightarrow{PQ}$ crosses circle Q, B.

2. Construct an arc with radius BQ and center A, which crosses $\overrightarrow{PQ}$ inside circle P; label the intersection point C. (PC is now the difference between the radii of the two circles.)

3. Draw the circle with center P and radius PC.

4. Find the midpoint of $\overline{PQ}$; label it D.

5. Draw the circle with center D and radius PD. Label the upper intersection of this circle and the circle of step #3, E. Draw tangent $\overline{EQ}$.

6. Draw ray $\overrightarrow{PE}$; label the point where it crosses the original circle P, F.

7. Draw an arc with center F and radius EQ that crosses circle Q; label the upper intersection point G.

8. EQGF now has both pairs of opposite sides equal and a right angle at E, so it is a rectangle. Therefore, $\overline{FG}$ is perpendicular to both radii $\overline{PF}$ and $\overline{QG}$; hence $\overline{FG}$ is the desired common external tangent.

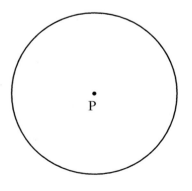

Lesson 9.6
Construct a Common Internal Tangent to Two Circles

If a belt around two pulleys followed the path of both external tangents, the pulleys would rotate in the same direction. But, if we want the pulleys to rotate in opposite directions, we must let the belt follow the path of the **common internal tangents,** one of which is shown to the right.

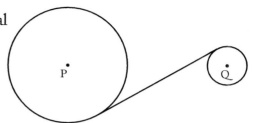

Your task is to figure out how to construct a common internal tangent to two circles. The procedure is very closely related to that of the common external tangent of Lesson 9.5. However, you will need to construct the *sum* of the radii of the two circles, rather than their difference.

Describe the steps of your construction below. (If a step is the same as in Lesson 9.5, just write "same." If a step is not the same, just tell how it is different.)

1. _____

2. _____

3. _____

4. _____

5. _____

6. _____

7. _____

8. _____

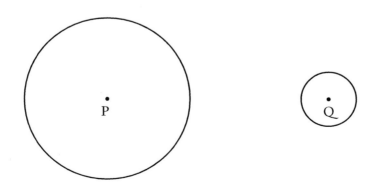

Chapter 10:
Construction Arithmetic

Lesson 10.1
Addition, Subtraction, and Constructing the Integers

The lessons in this chapter investigate which types of numbers and which arithmetic operations can be constructed with a straightedge and compass alone.

Positive real numbers are lengths of any and all segments. Special types of real numbers include the **positive integers** $(1, 2, 3, 4, \ldots)$ and the **positive rational numbers** (which can be written in the form $\frac{m}{n}$, where m and n are positive integers). There are many other real numbers that are not rational, such as $\sqrt{2}$ and π. We shall see which of these special types of numbers can be constructed and which cannot.

To these types of real numbers, we will try to apply various operations of arithmetic: addition, subtraction, multiplication, division, square root, and cube root. We shall see which of these operations can be constructed, and which cannot, with a straightedge and compass alone.

Let's begin with two real number lengths, x and y.

1. Starting at P, construct $\overline{PQ}$ that has length $x + y$. Label the endpoint Q.

P

2. Also construct $\overline{PR}$ that has length $x - y$. Label the endpoint R.

P

---

a. Given *any* two positive real numbers x and y, could you always construct their sum? (You might need a very long piece of paper!)

_____

b. Given *any* two unequal positive real numbers x and y, could you always construct their positive difference (larger minus smaller)?

_____

3. On the line below, a unit length 1 has been marked. Use repeated addition to construct lengths 2, 3, 4, 5, and 6. (Each length starts at P.) Label each arc as on a number line.

c. Given a unit length 1 (and a very long line!), describe how you could use repeated addition to construct *any* positive integer, *n*.

_____

_____

Our work thus far shows that, for any two real numbers, addition and subtraction are constructible, and that, given a unit length, we can use repeated addition to construct the positive integers.

Lesson 10.2
Multiplication by an Integer

Here is a positive integer, 4, and two real numbers, *x* and *y*.

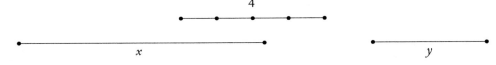

1. Starting at P, construct $\overline{PQ}$ that has length 3×4 (that is, 3 times as long as 4). Label the endpoint Q.

P

2. Starting at P, construct $\overline{PR}$ that has length $3 \times y$ (that is, 3 times as long as *y*). Label the endpoint R.

P

a. Given *any* two positive integers (and a very long line!), would it be possible to construct their product?

   _____

b. Given any real number *y* (and a very long line!), describe how you could use repeated addition to construct the product $4 \times y$.

   _____

   _____

c. Given any positive real number, *x*, and any positive integer, *n*, describe how you could use repeated addition to construct the product $n \times x$.

   _____

   _____

d. But, if neither *x* nor *y* is an integer, can you construct the product $x \times y$ using only repeated addition? Explain why or why not.

   _____

   _____

Lesson 10.3
Multiplication of Real Numbers

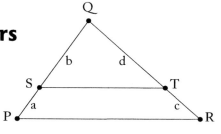

Given any two real numbers x and y, and given a segment of length 1, we can construct the product $x \times y$ using the Side-Splitter. This theorem states that, *if the sides of a triangle are split by a segment drawn parallel to the base, then the sides are split into proportional segments.* In the figure above, if $\overline{ST}$ is drawn parallel to $\overline{PR}$, then $\frac{a}{b} = \frac{c}{d}$. (Students of high school geometry are invited to prove the Side-Splitter Theorem in Appendix B.)

Follow these directions to construct $x \times y$ on the sides of angle Q below.

1. Locate point S on the left side such that QS = 1.

2. Locate P on the left side such that SP = x.

3. Locate T on the right side such that QT = y.

4. Draw $\overline{ST}$.

5. Draw an arc with radius ST and center P.

6. Draw an arc with radius SP and center T. Label the intersection of these arcs, W. (Do you see that PSTW is a parallelogram?)

7. Draw the ray $\overrightarrow{PW}$, which is parallel to $\overline{ST}$.

8. Label the point where $\overrightarrow{PW}$ intersects the right side of $\angle Q$, R.

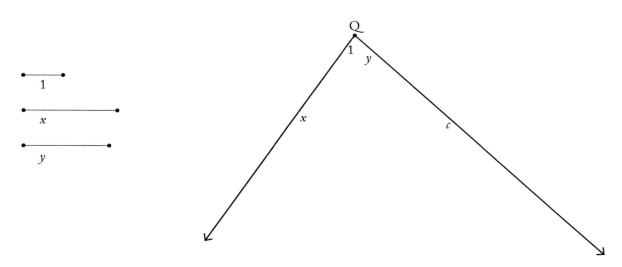

> a. Fit the lengths 1, x, y, and c into the proportion $\frac{a}{b} = \frac{c}{d}$. _____
>
> b. Solve the proportion for c. _____

This construction shows that multiplication is constructible for all real numbers.

Lesson 10.4
Euclidean Division Yielding Quotient and Remainder

In elementary school, one learns how to do division problems by finding an **integer quotient** and a **remainder**. For example, when 22 is divided by 5, the quotient is 4 and the remainder is 2. One also learns to check the answer by calculating whether $22 = 4 \times 5 + 2$.

$$5\overline{)22} \\ \frac{20}{2}$$

We will now *construct* the division $22 \div 5$, using repeated subtraction.

1. Construct more arcs to subtract as many 5s as you can from 22.

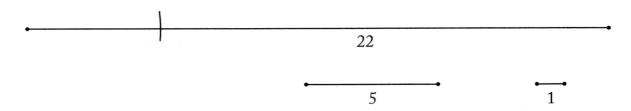

22

5   1

---

a. i. How many segments of length 5 will fit? _____

    ii. How long is the remaining piece? _____

---

2. Construct more arcs to divide $25 \div 7$ to obtain a quotient and a remainder.

25

7   1

---

b. Fill in the quotient and remainder into this equation: $25 = \underline{} \times 7 + \underline{}$.

c. Now imagine dividing $7 \div 25$. Fill in the quotient and remainder.
   (Hint: How many times does 25 go into 7?)

   $7 = \underline{} \times 25 + \underline{}$.

d. Fill in quotient and remainder for $32 \div 16$. $32 = \underline{} \times 16 + \underline{}$.

---

e. In general, for any positive integers n and d, when you divide $n \div d$ by repeated subtraction, you find integers q and r such that $n = q \times d + r$.

    i. What is the limit on how big r should be? _____

    ii. Could the remainder r possibly be 0? _____

    iii. Write an inequality that shows both restrictions on r. _____

3. Now consider division with *any* positive **real number** lengths x and y, *which might not be integers*. Construct arcs to subtract y repeatedly from x.

$$x$$

$$y$$

f. Considering your construction above, given *any* positive real numbers x and y, when you try to divide $x \div y$ using repeated subtraction,

    i. . . . would you be able to find an integer quotient, q? _____

    ii. . . . would the remaining piece certainly be an integer? _____

Lesson 10.5
Division Into an Integer Number of Parts

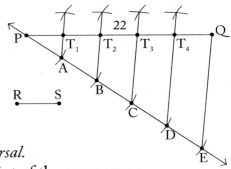

In the previous lesson, we divided 22 by 5 to obtain quotient 4 and remainder 2. Another way to interpret division would be to divide a segment of length 22 into 5 equal pieces. This form of division yields a **rational quotient**, $22 \div 5 = \frac{22}{5}$, with no remainder. To construct this quotient, we use the theorem that, *if parallel lines intercept congruent segments on one transversal, they intercept congruent segments on any other transversal.*

1. Open your compass to the length RS below. Place the point of the compass on P, and mark an arc across the oblique line. Label the intersection point A.

2. Mark off five more equally spaced arcs to obtain points B, C, D, and E.

3. Draw $\overline{EQ}$.

4. Construct a line parallel to $\overline{EQ}$ that passes through D. (To do this, draw an arc with center Q and radius DE, tending to the left of Q; draw an arc with center D and radius EQ that crosses the other arc; then draw a segment from the intersection of these arcs to point D. This intersection and points D, E, and Q are vertices of a parallelogram.) Label the point where the parallel line crosses $\overline{PQ}$, T_4.

5. In the same manner, construct other parallel lines that pass through C, B, and A. Label the points where these lines cross $\overline{PQ}$, T_3, T_2, and T_1.

6. The parallel lines divide $\overline{PQ}$ into five equal pieces; each piece has length $\frac{22}{5}$.

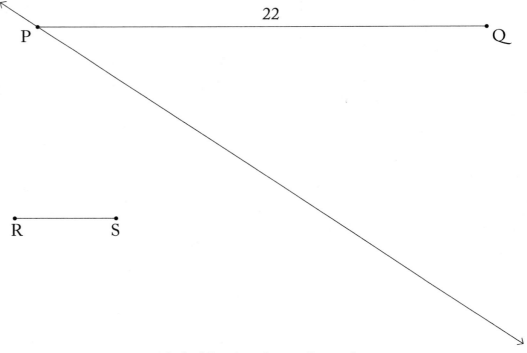

a. Could you use this method to divide *any* positive
real number, *x*, by *any* positive integer, *n*, to obtain $\frac{x}{n}$? _____

b. If you tried to divide *x* by a noninteger, *y*, to obtain $\frac{x}{y}$, what part of this procedure
would become troublesome?

_____

_____

Lesson 10.6
Constructing Rational Numbers

The segment $\overline{PQ}$ below has length 1. We will construct the rational number $\frac{3}{7}$, using a variation of the method of Lesson 10.5.

1. Using radius RS and starting at P, mark off seven arcs on the oblique line. Label the fourth arc D and the seventh arc G.

2. Draw an arc with radius GP and center Q; draw an arc with radius GQ and center P; label the point where the arcs cross, N. Connect the vertices of parallelogram PGQN.

3. Using radius RS and starting at Q, mark off three arcs on side $\overline{QN}$. Label the third arc, J.

4. Draw $\overline{DJ}$. Label the point where $\overline{DJ}$ intersects $\overline{PQ}$, T. Then TQ = $\frac{3}{7}$.

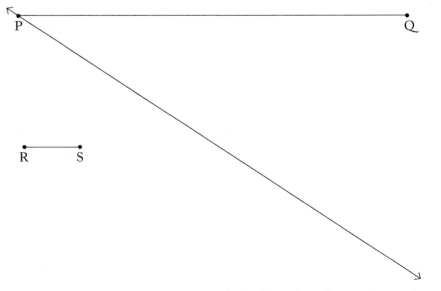

All positive **rational numbers** can be written in the form $\frac{m}{n}$, where m and n are positive integers. Would it be possible to use this method to construct *any* positive rational number $\frac{m}{n}$?

_____

Lesson 10.7
Division of Real Numbers

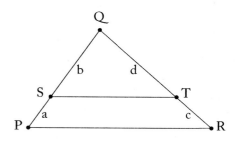

Given any two real numbers x and y, and given a segment of length 1, we can construct the quotient $\frac{x}{y}$ using the Side-Splitter Theorem. Applied to the figure nearby, this theorem tells us that, *if* $\overline{ST}$ *is parallel to* $\overline{PR}$, *then* $\frac{a}{b} = \frac{c}{d}$.

a. Solve the proportion for c. _____

b. Correlate a, b, and d with x, y, and 1 so that $c = \frac{x}{y}$. $a =$ _____ $b =$ _____ $d =$ _____

1. On the sides of angle Q below, locate and label points S, P, and T using the lengths you selected above, and the measurements below.

2. As you did in Lesson 10.3, construct a ray through P parallel to $\overline{ST}$. Label the point where this ray crosses $\overline{QT}$, R. Label $\overline{TR}$, $\frac{x}{y}$.

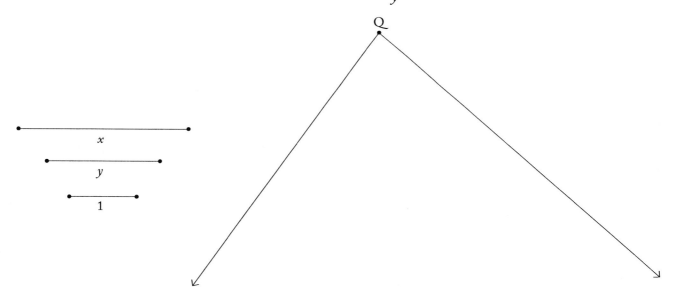

c. Use a ruler to measure x and y above. What is the ratio of $\frac{x}{y}$? _____

d. Use a ruler to measure the length of your segment $\frac{x}{y}$ and the length of "1" above. What is the ratio of $\frac{\frac{x}{y}}{1}$?

_____

e. Should the answers to questions c and d above be equal? _____

This construction shows that division is constructible for all real numbers.

Lesson 10.8
The Square Root Spiral

In Lesson 10.6, you found that it is possible to construct any rational number. It also is possible to construct some real numbers that are not rational. Starting with a segment of length 1, it is possible to construct the positive **square root** of any positive integer using the Square Root Spiral.

The Pythagorean Theorem tells us that *if x and y are lengths of the legs of a right triangle and z is the length of its hypotenuse, then z = $\sqrt{x^2 + y^2}$*. In particular, if *x* and *y* both happen to be 1, then the hypotenuse will be $\sqrt{2}$. We will construct a spiral of right triangles with hypotenuses $\sqrt{2}, \sqrt{3}, \sqrt{4}, \sqrt{5}$, and so on. Using the triangle on the next page, follow the steps below.

1. Label the length OB below as $\sqrt{2}$.

2. Extend $\overrightarrow{OB}$ beyond B.

3. Erect a line perpendicular to $\overrightarrow{OB}$ through B. (Use the method of Lesson 4.1.)

4. Open your compass radius to AB (which is 1). Put the center on B, and mark an arc across the perpendicular line. Label the intersection point C. Label CB, 1.

5. Draw $\overline{OC}$. ΔOBC now has legs of lengths 1 and $\sqrt{2}$. By the Pythagorean Theorem, its hypotenuse will be $\sqrt{1^2 + \sqrt{2}^2}$, which is $\sqrt{1+2}$; so label $\overline{OC}$ as $\sqrt{3}$.

6. Erect a line perpendicular to $\overline{OC}$ through C.

7. Open your compass radius to AB. Put the center on C, and mark an arc across the perpendicular line. Label the intersection point D. Label CD, 1.

8. Draw $\overline{OD}$, and label it $\sqrt{4}$. ($\overline{OD}$ should be twice as long as $\overline{OA}$.)

9. Continue in this way to construct segments with lengths $\sqrt{5}, \sqrt{6}$, and $\sqrt{7}$.

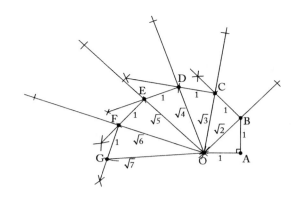

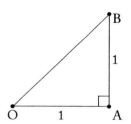

© **Prufrock Press Inc.** • *Compass Constructions*

This page may be photocopied or reproduced with permission for classroom use only.

95

Lesson 10.9
Construct the Square Root of Any Positive Real Number

Given *any* real number, *x*, and a segment of length 1, it is possible to construct a segment with length $\sqrt{x}$.

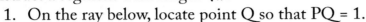

1. On the ray below, locate point Q so that PQ = 1.
2. On the ray below, locate point R to the right of Q, so that QR = *x*.
3. Construct the perpendicular bisector of $\overline{PR}$. Label the midpoint of $\overline{PR}$, M.
4. Construct the circle with center M and passing through P.
5. Label the top point where the perpendicular bisector crosses the circle, T. (We will use $\overline{TM}$ in Lesson 10.10.)
6. Erect a line through Q perpendicular to $\overline{PR}$. (Use the method of Lesson 4.1.)
7. Label the point where this perpendicular crosses the circle, S.
8. Draw $\overline{PS}$ and $\overline{SR}$.

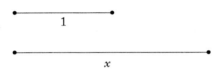

a. Why is ∠PSR a right angle?

_____

_____

b. Which small triangle is similar to ΔPQS? _____

c. What proportion can be written involving 1, SQ, and *x*? _____

d. What is the length SQ? _____

Lesson 10.10
Construct the Arithmetic and Geometric Means

Given any two positive real numbers x and y, it is possible to construct their **arithmetic mean** (or **average**), $\frac{x+y}{2}$, and their **geometric mean**, $\sqrt{xy}$. You already have constructed both the arithmetic mean and the geometric mean of x and 1. Look back at Lesson 10.9.

a. Which vertical segment has length $\frac{x+1}{2}$, the arithmetic mean? _____

b. Which vertical segment has length $\sqrt{x \cdot 1}$, the geometric mean? _____

Now, generalize the method of Lesson 10.9 to construct both the arithmetic mean and the geometric mean of lengths x and y below. On your construction, label x, y, and points Q, R, M, T, and S. Also label which vertical segment is the arithmetic mean and which is the geometric mean.

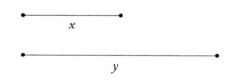

x

y

P

c. Draw $\overline{SM}$. Which is longer $\overline{SQ}$ or $\overline{SM}$, and why?

_____

d. Which is longer, $\overline{SM}$ or $\overline{TM}$, and why?

_____

e. Which of these two means is always less than or equal to the other, and why?

_____

Lesson 10.11
Construct the Harmonic Mean

Given any two positive real numbers x and y, their **harmonic mean** h is $\frac{1}{\frac{1}{x}+\frac{1}{y}}$. In other words, h satisfies the relationship $\frac{1}{h}=\frac{1}{x}+\frac{1}{y}$. To construct the harmonic mean of x and y, follow the steps below.

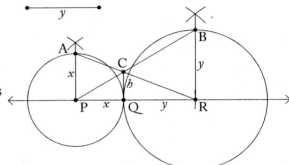

1. Construct a circle with radius x and center P. Label the right point where the circle intersects the line, Q. Label length PQ = x.

2. Draw an arc with radius y and center Q, to the right of Q. Label the point where the arc crosses the line, R. Label length QR = y.

3. Draw the circle with radius y and center R.

4. Erect a perpendicular at P.

5. Label the point where the perpendicular intersects circle P, A. Label AP, x.

6. Erect a perpendicular at R.

7. Label the point where this perpendicular intersects circle R, B. Label BR, y.

8. Draw $\overline{AR}$ and $\overline{BP}$. Label the point where $\overline{AR}$ intersects $\overline{BP}$, C.

9. Draw $\overline{CQ}$ and label it h. $\overline{CQ}$ is the harmonic mean of x and y.

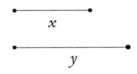

a. (Extra Credit.) Explain how to prove that $\triangle APR \sim \triangle CQR$.

b. Using the fact that $\triangle APR \sim \triangle CQR$, use algebra to show that $\overline{CQ}$ really is the harmonic mean of x and y.

c. The harmonic mean has practical applications. If you travel from one place to another at an average speed x, and you return at an average speed y, then your average speed for the entire trip is twice the harmonic mean of x and y.

Suppose Karen Driver drives from home to work at an average speed of 30 mph, but slow traffic on the way home reduces her average speed to 20 mph. What is Karen's average speed for the round trip?

d. Another practical application involves resistors wired in parallel. If two resistors are wired in parallel, then the harmonic mean of the two resistances is the total resistance of the circuit.

Suppose two light bulbs are wired in parallel and connected to a battery. One bulb has resistance 8 ohms, the other 4 ohms. What is the total resistance of the circuit?

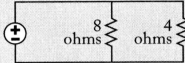

e. Look back at your construction of the harmonic mean. How do you suppose the harmonic mean compares in size to the geometric mean and the arithmetic mean?

f. (Extra Credit.) Prove which is smaller, the harmonic or the geometric mean.

Lesson 10.12
What Can You Not Construct?

The ancient Greek geometers proposed three constructions that they could not accomplish in a finite number of steps using just a straightedge and compass. In the ensuing 2,000 years, all three classic constructions have been shown to be impossible without at least some markings on the straightedge.

1. Squaring the Circle.

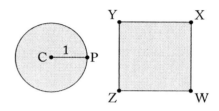

Given a circle, using just a straightedge and compass, it is not possible to construct a square with the same area.

Because the area of a circle is $A = \pi r^2$, the area of a circle with radius 1 is π. For a square to have area π, its side must be $\sqrt{\pi}$. We have seen that we could construct $\sqrt{\pi}$ if and only if we could construct π. But, in 1882, more than 2,300 years after the Greeks posed the question, Ferdinand von Lindemann proved that π was transcendental and that it cannot be constructed in a finite number of steps with straightedge and compass.

You can construct a curved form of π: If the diameter of a circle is 1, its circumference has length π. However, we would need a straight segment with length π in order to "square the circle."

2. Trisecting an Angle

Given any angle, using just a straightedge and compass, it is not possible to divide the angle into three congruent angles.

Some angles *can* be trisected; for example, it is easy to split a 90° angle into three 30° angles. What we would want is a method that would work to trisect *any* given angle.

In Lesson 10.5, you learned a method that could be used to trisect a segment into three equal lengths. But, in the trisection shown nearby, points A, W, X, and C are equally spaced around a *circle*—not equally spaced on a segment.

In 1836, Pierre Wantzel proved that it is impossible to find a method of trisecting an angle with straightedge and compass alone.

3. **Doubling the Cube**

According to ancient legend, plague struck Athens in 430 BC. The Athenians consulted the Oracle on the Island of Delos, birthplace of Apollo. The Oracle advised them to double the size of the altar of Apollo, a task they promptly undertook. The plague continuing, they realized they had erred by doubling each *edge* of the cube, thereby multiplying its volume by eight. To double the *volume*, they would need to construct a cube with edge length $\sqrt[3]{2}$ times as long as the original edge. They were unable to accomplish this task. Constructing a cube root was proved impossible, again by Wantzel, in 1836.

Wantzel's methods also demonstrate the impossibility of constructing a regular heptagon with just a straightedge and compass.

Appendices

Appendix A: Proof of Properties of Kites

If you are a student of high school geometry, you can prove the three basic properties of kites. Fill in the blanks in the proof below.

Given: $\overline{KI} \cong \overline{TI}$; $\overline{KE} \cong \overline{TE}$

Prove:
1. $\overline{EI}$ bisects $\angle KET$,
2. M is the midpoint of $\overline{KT}$, and
3. $\overline{IE}$ is the perpendicular bisector of $\overline{KT}$.

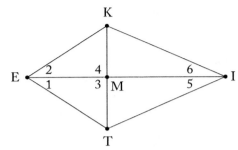

Proof:

1. $\overline{KI} \cong \overline{TI}$; $\overline{KE} \cong \overline{TE}$	1. Given
2. _____	2. Reflexive
3. $\triangle KIE \cong \triangle TIE$	3. _____
4. $\angle 1 \cong \angle 2$	4. CPCTC
5. _____	5. If a ray divides an angle into two $\cong$ angles, then it bisects the angle.
6. $\overline{EM} \cong \overline{EM}$	6. _____
7. _____	7. SAS
8. $\overline{KM} \cong \overline{MT}$	8. _____
9. _____	9. If a point divides a segment into two $\cong$ segments, then it is the midpoint.
10. $\angle 3 \cong \angle 4$	10. _____
11. $m\angle 3 + m\angle 4 = 180$	11. _____
12. $2 \cdot m\angle 3 = 180$	12. Substitution $10 \rightarrow 11$
13. $m\angle 3 = 90$	13. _____
14. $\overline{EI} \perp \overline{KT}$	14. _____
15. _____	15. If a segment is perpendicular to another segment and contains its midpoint, then it is the perpendicular bisector.

Appendix B: Proof of the Side-Splitter Theorem

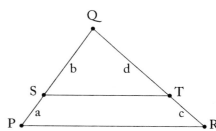

Given: $\triangle PQR$
$\overline{ST}$ parallel to $\overline{PR}$

Prove: $\dfrac{a}{b} = \dfrac{c}{d}$

Proof:

1. $\overline{ST}$ parallel to $\overline{PR}$	1. Given
2. $\angle QST \cong \angle QPR \quad \angle QTS \cong \angle QRP$	2. _____
3. $\triangle QPR$ is similar to $\triangle QST$	3. _____
4. $\dfrac{a+b}{b} = \dfrac{c+d}{d}$	4. _____
5. $\dfrac{a}{b} + \underline{\quad} = \dfrac{c}{d} + \underline{\quad}$	5. Adding Fractions (used in reverse)
6. $\dfrac{a}{b} = \dfrac{c}{d}$	6. _____

Appendix C:
Hilbert's Theorem That All Triangles Are Isosceles

The mathematician David Hilbert proposed the following "proof" that all triangles are isosceles. Can you find its flaw? (Hint: Make your own construction.)

Given: △HIL
Prove: △HIL is isosceles
Proof:

1. Construct the ⊥ bis of $\overline{IL}$ at midpt B	1. Construction
2. Construct the ∠ bis of ∠IHL	2. Construction
3. Call their intersection point R	3. Construction
4. Drop $\overline{RE} \perp \overline{HI}$ and $\overline{RT} \perp \overline{HL}$	4. Construction
5. ∠IHR ≅ ∠LHR	5. Definition angle bisector
6. ∠REH and ∠RTH are right angles	6. Perpendiculars form right angles.
7. ∠REH ≅ ∠RTH	7. All right angles are congruent.
8. $\overline{HR} \cong \overline{HR}$	8. Reflexive
9. △REH ≅ △RTH	9. SAA (steps 8, 7, 5)
10. $\overline{RE} \cong \overline{RT}$	10. CPCTC
11. $\overline{RI} \cong \overline{RL}$	11. Every point on a ⊥ bisector of a segment is equidistant from its endpoints.
12. △REI ≅ △RTL	12. HL (steps 11, 10, 6)
13. $\overline{IE} \cong \overline{LT}$	13. CPCTC
14. $\overline{EH} \cong \overline{TH}$	14. CPCTC (step 9)
15. $\overline{IH} \cong \overline{LH}$	15. Subtraction
16. △HIL is isosceles	16. Definition of isosceles

Q.E.D.???

Answers

Lesson 1.3
B is the center.

Lesson 2.2
The diagonals of a nonconvex kite do not
   intersect.

Lesson 2.3
   a. Right
   b. Equal
   c. Equal
   d. Equal

Lesson 3.5
Two

Lesson 3.6
   a. Two
   b. The nine points are: three midpoints,
      three altitudes' feet, and three points
      midway from a foot to the orthocenter.

Lesson 4.3
Opposite sides of a rectangle are parallel and
   equal in length.

Lesson 4.4
The diagonals of a rectangle are equal, and
   they bisect each other.

Lesson 4.5
   a. A possible method:
      2. Open the compass to radius DC.
      3. Draw an arc with center D; label the
         point where the arc crosses m, A.
      4. Draw an arc with center A to the right
         of A.
      5. Draw an arc with center C above C.
      6. Label the point where the arcs cross, B.
      7. Draw ABCD.
   b. A square's diagonals are equal in length,
      are perpendicular to each other, bisect
      each other, and bisect the angles of the
      square.

Lesson 5.4
   a. Yes
   b. Yes
   c. Yes
   d. Yes
   e. Yes
   f. ii
   g. No
   h. No
   i. No
   j. Yes

Lesson 5.6
   1. Draw arc with radius PS and center R.
   2. Draw arc with radius SR and center P.
   3. Label the point where the two arcs cross,
      Q.
   4. Draw PQRS.

Lesson 6.1
   a. Flip it over side 3.
   b. Yes, because one will fit on top of the
      other.
   c. Yes, because the two triangles you can
      construct are not different.
   d. Yes
   e. Side 3 is too long, so side 1 and side 2
      can't reach each other.
   f. It must be that side 3 < side 1 + side 2
   g. Yes

Lesson 6.2
   a. Kite
   b. Three
   c. Parallelogram
   d. Three
   e. The midsegment is half as long as the side
      it is parallel to.
   f. The grey triangle has one quarter the area
      of the white triangle.
   g. An isosceles trapezoid is formed.

Lesson 6.4
   a. The rays don't intersect.
   b. No

c. 180°. Because the sum of all three angles of a triangle is 180°, the sum of any two angles must be less than 180°.

d. Yes

Lesson 6.5

a. Yes

b. Yes

c. No, the construction method will work for any side lengths.

d. Yes, as long as the angle is between 0° and 180°.

Lesson 6.6

a. Yes

b. Yes

c. Make side 2 longer than side 1.

d. SsA determines a triangle whenever the side opposite the angle is bigger than the side adjacent to the angle; in SsA, the S opposite the A is bigger than the s next to the A.

e. Yes

f. No

g. No

h. Yes

i. Yes

j. Yes

k. Two

l. No

m. Yes

n. Angle C is a right angle.

o. Yes

p. No

q. No

r. SSA determines a triangle when . . .

　i. opposite > adjacent and the angle is obtuse, right, or acute.

　ii. opposite = adjacent and the angle is acute.

　iii. opposite < adjacent, the angle is acute.

　iv. The triangle formed is a right triangle.

Lesson 7.1

They are parallel and the midsegment is half as long as the base.

Lesson 7.2

a. MNOP is a parallelogram.

b. $\overline{MN}$

c. $\overline{OP}$

d. As midsegments, both $\overline{MN}$ and $\overline{OP}$ are parallel to $\overline{AC}$, so they are parallel to each other.

e. Both $\overline{MN}$ and $\overline{OP}$ are half as long as $\overline{AC}$, so they are the same length.

f. Because MNOP has two opposite sides that are parallel and equal, MNOP must be a parallelogram.

Lesson 7.3

a. a rhombus

b. a rectangle

Lesson 7.5

a. Answers will vary; about 1.6.

b. $\phi = \frac{1+\sqrt{5}}{2}$

Lesson 8.1

a. The arc crosses inside angle W.

b. To be congruent, the arc should cross *on* the side of the angle.

c. $\angle Y \cong \angle V$. Angles W and Z are too large, and angle X is too small.

Lesson 8.2

a. Yes, $\angle C \cong \angle C'$

b. $\frac{3}{1}$

c. $\frac{3}{1}$ and $\frac{3}{1}$.

Lesson 8.3

a. All are $\frac{1}{2}$.

b. All are $\frac{2}{1}$.

c. Yes, and all the other corresponding angles are also congruent.

d. Yes, all three triangles are similar.

Lesson 8.4

a. Because both pairs of opposite sides are congruent, PRCB is a parallelogram.

b. If lines are parallel, then corresponding angles are $\cong$.

d. $\triangle ABC \sim \triangle APQ \sim \triangle CRQ$ by AA~.

e. $\frac{AP}{AB} = \frac{AQ}{AC} = \frac{PQ}{BC}$ & $\frac{CR}{AB} = \frac{CQ}{AC} = \frac{RQ}{BC}$.

Lesson 8.5

a. Drop a perpendicular from C, that intersects $\overline{AB}$ at D.

b. i. $\triangle I$ is $\triangle ACD$; $\triangle II$ is $\triangle CBD$.

   ii. $\angle A \cong \angle BCD$.

   iii. $\angle B \cong \angle ACD$.

c. $\triangle ABC \sim \triangle ACD \sim \triangle CBD$.

d. The triangles are similar by AA ~.

e. $\frac{AD}{CD} = \frac{CD}{BD}$

Lesson 9.1

a. Right angle

b. Right angle

c. Any angle inscribed in a semicircle is a right angle.

Lesson 9.2

1. Construct the midpoint M of $\overline{AC}$.

2. Draw the circle with center M passing through A.

3. Draw arc with radius side 1 and center A, above A. Label the point where the arc crosses the circle, point B.

4. Draw arc with radius side 1 and center C, below C. Label the point where the arc crosses the circle, point D.

5. Connect ABCD.

Lesson 9.3

1. Draw ray $\overrightarrow{OP}$.

2. Draw an arc with radius OP and center P; label the point where this arc crosses ray $\overrightarrow{OP}$, A.

3. Using a larger radius, construct arcs with centers O and A.

4. Label the point where these arcs cross, B.

5. Draw $\overleftrightarrow{PB}$, which is tangent to the circle.

Lesson 9.4

1. Draw $\overline{OP}$

2. Construct the midpoint M of $\overline{OP}$.

3. Draw the circle with center M and passing through O.

4. Label either point where the circles cross, point T.

5. Draw tangent $\overline{PT}$.

Lesson 9.6

The steps are identical to those in Lesson 9.5, except in Step 2, the point C should be *outside* circle P so that PC is the *sum* of the radii of the two circles, Step 5, label the *lower* intersection point E, and Step 8, you have constructed the common *internal* tangent.

Lesson 10.1

a. Yes

b. Yes

c. To construct any positive integer *n*, add together *n* copies of the unit length.

Lesson 10.2

a. Yes; one integer tells you how many copies of the other integer to add together.

b. To construct $4 \times y$, add together four copies of y.

c. To construct $n \times x$, add together n copies of x.

d. No, because you can't tell how many copies of either x or y to add together.

Lesson 10.3

a. $\dfrac{x}{1} = \dfrac{c}{y}$

b. $c = xy$

Lesson 10.4

a. i. 4

  ii. 2

b. $25 = 3 \times 7 + 4$

c. $7 = 0 \times 25 + 7$

d. $32 = 2 \times 16 + 0$

e. i. $r < d$

  ii. Yes

  iii. $0 \le r < d$

f. i. Yes

  ii. No

Lesson 10.5

a. Yes

b. You can't tell how many copies to make along the oblique ray.

Lesson 10.6

a. Yes. (If $m > n$, you could either extend ray $\overrightarrow{QN}$ to have room to make enough copies of $\overline{RS}$, or rewrite $\dfrac{m}{n}$ as a mixed number and construct the integer part and fraction part separately.)

Lesson 10.7

a. $c = \dfrac{ad}{b}$

b. $a = x$ (or 1)

  $b = y$

  $c = 1$ (or x)

c. 1.5

d. 1.5

e. Yes

Lesson 10.9

a. Any angle inscribed in a semicircle is a right angle.

b. $\triangle SQR$

c. $\dfrac{1}{SQ} = \dfrac{SQ}{x}$

d. $SQ = \sqrt{x}$

Lesson 10.10

a. $\overline{TM}$

b. $\overline{SQ}$

c. $SQ \le SM$, because the shortest distance from a point to a line is measured along the perpendicular segment.

d. $SM = TM$, because all radii of a circle are equal in length.

e. Because $SQ \le SM = TM$, the geometric mean is less than or equal to the arithmetic mean.

Lesson 10.11

a. $\overline{PA} \parallel \overline{RB}$, because both are perpendicular to $\overline{PR}$. Because parallel lines imply alternate interior angles $\cong$, $\triangle APC \sim \triangle RBC$ by AA~. Because corresponding sides of similar triangles are proportional, $\dfrac{AC}{CR} = \dfrac{x}{y}$. Then $\triangle APR \sim \triangle CQR$ by the Converse Side-Splitter Theorem.

b. Let $h = CQ$. Because corresponding parts of similar triangles are proportional, $\dfrac{h}{x} = \dfrac{y}{x+y}$. Multiplying both sides by x, we have $h = \dfrac{xy}{x+y}$. Taking the reciprocal of each side, we have $\dfrac{1}{h} = \dfrac{x+y}{xy} = \dfrac{1}{x} + \dfrac{1}{y}$.

c. $\dfrac{1}{h} = \dfrac{1}{30} + \dfrac{1}{20} = \dfrac{50}{600} = \dfrac{1}{12}$; $h = 12$;

  $2h = 24$ mph.

d. $\dfrac{1}{h} = \dfrac{1}{8} + \dfrac{1}{4} = \dfrac{12}{32} = \dfrac{3}{8}$; $h = \dfrac{8}{3} \approx 2.7$ ohms

e. The harmonic mean is smaller than the geometric mean.

f. Algebraic proof:

For any $x > 0$, $y > 0$,

$$0 < x^2 + xy + y^2$$

$$xy < x^2 + 2xy + y^2$$

$$\frac{xy}{x^2 + 2xy + y^2} < 1$$

$$\frac{x^2 y^2}{x^2 + 2xy + y^2} < xy$$

$$\frac{xy}{x + y} < \sqrt{xy}$$

Appendix A

2. $\overline{EI} \cong \overline{EI}$
3. SSS
5. $\overline{EI}$ bisects $\angle KET$.
6. Reflexive
7. $\triangle KEM \cong \triangle TEM$
8. CPCTC
9. M is the midpoint of $\overline{KT}$.
10. CPCTC
11. Angle Addition
13. Multiplication Property of Equality
14. If two segments intersect in a right angle, then they are perpendicular.
15. $\overline{IE}$ is the perpendicular bisector of $\overline{KT}$.

Appendix B

2. If two parallel lines are cut by a transversal, then corresponding angles are congruent.
3. AA Similarity
4. Corresponding sides of similar triangles are proportional.
5. $\dfrac{a}{b} + \dfrac{b}{b} = \dfrac{c}{d} + \dfrac{d}{d}$
6. Subtraction Property of Equality

Appendix C

The flaw is in the diagram. If correctly constructed, either E lies on $\overline{HI}$ or T lies on $\overline{HL}$, but not both. Hence the line 15 of the proof cannot be justified by "subtraction," by "addition," or in any other way.